Dwarf Shrubs for the Midwest

Rebecca McIntosh Keith

F.A. Giles

University of Illinois Press

Urbana   Chicago   London

Edited by Richard Moores
Designed by Paula Wheeler
Drawings by F.A. Giles

Also published as Special Publication 60,
College of Agriculture, University of Illinois
at Urbana-Champaign

LIBRARY OF CONGRESS CATALOGING IN PUBLICATION DATA

Keith, Rebecca.
    Dwarf shrubs for the Midwest.

    "Also published as Special publication 60, College
of Agriculture, University of Illinois at Urbana-
Champaign."
    1. Dwarf shrubs — Middle West.   I. Giles, Floyd,
joint author.   II. Title.
SB435.52.M5K44   635.9′76′0977   80-12867
ISBN 0-252-00817-0

Preface

With constantly accelerating prices of land, construction, and financing, suburban houses are being built on increasingly smaller lots. Homeowners with large lots have discovered that trained labor is both expensive and scarce, and that it is time-consuming to maintain the grounds themselves. For these reasons, the trend today is toward using plants that require less maintenance and that are in scale with the contemporary home — the dwarf shrubs. One of the purposes of this book is to encourage the use of dwarf and small shrubs in the home landscape.

Although written primarily for home gardeners, **Dwarf Shrubs for the Midwest** may be equally useful to nursery or garden center operators, landscape contractors, landscape architects, teachers, and students. The book is divided into two main sections: (1) an introductory section containing general cultural information; and (2) detailed descriptions of 104 dwarf and small plants, including the botanical, common, and obsolete names of each plant, the hardiness zone in which the plant performs best, and uses of the plant in the home landscape. Each description is accompanied by a photograph of the plant (including 33 in full color) and line drawings of the leaves, stems, flowers, or fruits. The book also contains detailed cultural instructions for rhododendrons and dwarf conifers, an illustrated glossary of botanical terms, a list of publications for further reference, and an index of botanical and common names.

The plants described in this book were selected on the basis of the following general criteria: (1) adaptability to the climatic conditions and soils of the Midwest; (2) usefulness in the home landscape; (3) relative freedom from insects and diseases; (4) size (most of the plants do not exceed 4 feet in height); and (5) availability from retail nurseries, garden centers, and mail-order sources in the United States.

Although many professional architects no longer employ the term "foundation planting," we have retained it in this book because it is readily understood by readers. The English system of weights and measures is used throughout because most home gardeners have not yet adopted the metric system.

A book of this scope could not have been written without the help of many people. The authors particularly wish to thank the following: Professors John B. Gartner, James W. Gerdemann, Barry Jacobsen, Joseph C. McDaniel, William R. Nelson, Jr., Roscoe Randell, and David J. Williams of the University of Illinois at Urbana-Champaign; Robert A. Chamness, Belle Valley Nursery, Belleville, Illinois; Professor Michael A. Dirr, University of Georgia, Athens, Georgia; Robert Doren and Erik Neuman of the U.S. National Arboretum, Washington, D.C.; Henry Eilers, H.&E. Nursery, Litchfield, Illinois; Professor Harrison Flint, Purdue University, West Lafayette, Indiana; Justin C. Harper, horticulturist, John Deere Company, Moline, Illinois; Clarence Hubbuch, horticulturist, Bernheim Forest (Arboretum), Clermont, Kentucky; Professor Clancy Lewis, Michigan State University, East Lansing, Michigan; Ralph Little, Thornapple Nursery, Geneva, Illinois; John Neumann, Hickory Grove Nursery, Geneseo, Illinois; Wayne B. Siefert, area extension adviser, horticulture, Edwardsville, Illinois; Ralph Synnestvedt and Ralph Synnestvedt, Jr., Burr Oak Nursery, Glenview, Illinois; Charles Tosovsky, Home Nursery, Edwardsville, Illinois; and Don Zaun, Wasco, Illinois. We are especially grateful to Floyd Swink of the Morton Arboretum, Lisle, Illinois, for his meticulous review of plant nomenclature.

Rebecca McIntosh Keith
F.A. Giles

For my husband, Dale, and my children, Michael and Michelle, whose encouragement, patience, and sacrifices made this book possible.

R.M.K.

For Professor J.C. McDaniel, outstanding plantsman.

F.A.G.

Contents

Growing Dwarf and Small Shrubs

Plant Descriptions

Deciduous Shrubs

Broad-Leaved Evergreens

Rhododendron

Needle Evergreens (Dwarf Conifers)

r

Growing
Dwarf and Small Shrubs

There are many places in which dwarf plants can be used to advantage in the home landscape. Dwarf shrubs can provide a spectacular display in a sequence of flowering in the spring and summer, ornamental fruits, brilliant fall colors, and an interesting winter character. These plants range in habit from prostrate, to rounded, to upright, to pyramidal forms.

Many dwarf **deciduous** shrubs (plants whose leaves fall off at the end of each growing season) add flowers, fruits, autumn coloration, and a variety of foliage textures to the landscape. Some shrubs have ornamental bark or branching habits that are attractive during the winter. Pruning is usually simple or unnecessary.

Evergreens are plants that retain their leaves throughout the year. They lose part of their older foliage after the new foliage has matured. Some varieties of *Ilex opaca* (American holly), a broad-leaved evergreen, drop up to ⅔ of their leaves in the spring. *Pinus* (pine) species, which are conifers, drop many of their older needles in the autumn.

Evergreens may be divided into **broad-leaved evergreens** and **needle evergreens** (conifers). The broad-leaved evergreens represent many plant families, and often have conspicuous flowers, ornamental fruits, and attractive autumn coloration. This group includes the *Buxus* (boxwood), *Ilex* (hollies), and *Rhododendron* (rhododendrons and azaleas). Some of the plants in this group require special growing conditions.

The needle evergreens are conifers (cone-bearers), although not all conifers are evergreen. Some conifers — *Ginkgo biloba* (ginkgo tree), *Metasequoia* (dawn redwood), *Larix* (larch), and *Taxodium* (bald cypress) — are deciduous.

All conifers are not "green." There are many variations of green from yellow-green to gray-green to blue-green to black-green. Certain conifers undergo seasonal color changes. For example, some of the juniper species become plum-colored in the winter.

The foliage of some other junipers and certain *Picea* (spruce) is steel-blue, and the foliage of a few of the *Chamaecyparis* (false cypress) is a rich, golden hue. Because these vibrant colors create a focal point in the landscape, the plants should be used in moderation.

Conifers provide a sense of permanence and continuity to the landscape, especially during the winter when the deciduous plants are bare. The large, pyramidal conifers are difficult to incorporate into the flat Midwestern landscape, but the dwarf and slow-growing forms are becoming increasingly popular in foundation plantings, borders, permanent landscape containers, and rock gardens.

The advantages of using dwarf shrubs in the landscape are that they provide permanence and four-seasonal interest, do not outgrow their locations, and require little maintenance.

Unfortunately, many homeowners become short-sighted when they can purchase several fast-growing shrubs for the price of one dwarf shrub, even though the dwarf shrub may be a better long-term investment. For this reason, nursery owners are often reluctant to grow dwarf shrubs.

How Dwarf Shrubs Originate

Many dwarf plants are naturally low growing, such as *Daphne cneorum, Juniperus procumbens, Mahonia repens,* and *Cotoneaster horizontalis.* These plants can be propagated from seed. The seedlings retain the characteristics of the parents.

Dwarf plants may also occur as the result of seedling variation. Some plants grown from seed show distinct variation from the typical species in one or more characteristics: size, habit (fastigiate, weeping, globose, etc.), growth rate, hardiness, and the color, size, or shape of the leaf, flower, fruit, or stem. These seedling forms are generally stable, and do not revert to the growth habit of the original species. The plants must be propagated asexually or vegetatively to maintain these characteristics. Often the plants showing the variation (notably the dwarf coniferous species) set sterile seed.

Occasionally new forms of dwarf conifers (for example, false cypress and junipers) result from the propagation of a branch with juvenile (awl-shaped)

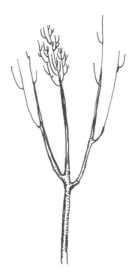

Witches'-broom
(deciduous plant)

Witches'-broom
(evergreen plant)

leaves. The resulting plant usually has only the juvenile foliage, but may revert to the adult form of the parent plant. Reverted branches should be removed as soon as possible.

New types, such as plants with variegated leaves, occur as "sports" or bud mutations. These plants must be vegetatively propagated to maintain the new form. Witchs'-broom, a bud mutation, is an abnormal development of a cluster of dense, stunted branchlets. It may be induced by fungi, dwarf mistletoe, a virus, insects, or mites. Cuttings or grafts from witchs'-broom result in dwarf plants such as *Picea abies* 'Pygmaea'. Bud mutations tend to revert to the parent plant.

Diminutive conifers are often derived by selecting the cuttings from weak-growing shoots near the bottom of the plant. The plant fails to develop a central leader and grows very slowly. In old age, however, the plant may begin to grow rapidly.

A graft, collected from wood on the side branches of many conifers, produces a plant with a horizontal habit. These plants may be quite small or rather large. If damaged, the plant may suddenly develop an upright leader. This leader should be removed immediately; otherwise, a "monstrous" plant results and the horizontal effect is lost.

How to Use Dwarf Shrubs in the Home Landscape

The first step towards developing an aesthetically pleasing landscape is to prepare a plan on paper. This plan should show permanent structures and plantings, as well as property lines drawn to scale. Carefully note the locations of utilities, problem areas (objectionable views on or off the property, low, wet spots, etc.), and positive characteristics (a pleasing view on or off the property, a stream running through the property, a rock outcropping, etc.). Taking these features into consideration before working out the planting details will help you to develop an attractive landscape.

Plants are displayed to their best advantage when grouped and placed in "beds" that are sharply distinguished from the lawn areas. Frequently home gardeners place shrubs separately or in isolated spots in the lawn area, creating a "shotgun" effect. This effect is not only visually disrupting, but the plants must compete with lawn grasses for water and nutrients, maintenance is more difficult, and they are easily damaged by lawn mowers. A carefully conceived plan, including the choice of the correct plants for the site, eliminates many problems that could arise later.

The homegrounds consists of three basic areas: the public area, the outdoor living area, and the service or utility area. Dwarf shrubs can be successfully used in the public area and the outdoor living area.

The **public area** is the space between the house and the street that is visible to the public. The house is the most important element in this area. The landscape should enhance the house by accentuating its positive structural features and masking any awkward ones.

The foundation planting seeks to blend the harsh, vertical, architectural lines of the house with the soft, horizontal lines of the landscape through interesting, carefully designed plantings. These plantings are most effective when they consist of a combination of conifers, deciduous shrubs, and broad-leaved evergreens so that the effect of the foundation planting changes with the seasons. Dwarf plants can be effectively placed in the foundation planting because they will not outgrow their intended space.

The **outdoor living area** is usually the area behind the house. It should be designed to fit the family's outdoor living needs: patio, barbeque pit, space for lawn games, play areas for children, flower or vegetable gardens, etc. Dwarf shrubs may be used in this area as (1) specimen plants; (2) in front of the taller growing shrubs in the shrub border; (3) combined with flowers in the flower bed; (4) to edge a walk or drive; and (5) in front of a fence or near the garage to blend these structures with the ground.

The addition of a few well-chosen dwarf shrubs gives interest, variation, and substance to the flower border during the winter. In the spring and summer, the dwarf plants provide an interesting low background for bulbs, perennials, and annuals.

Many of the dwarf shrubs can serve as specimen plants. These plants are chosen on the basis of their four-seasonal appeal, and are used to draw attention to a particular spot in the landscape.

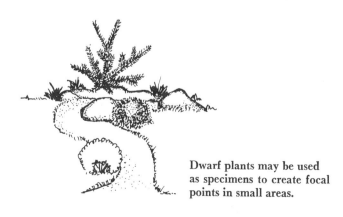

Dwarf plants may be used as specimens to create focal points in small areas.

Dwarf plants may also be used to control traffic patterns without obstructing visibility. A well-chosen plant or a mass planting can direct people around an object or prevent them from rounding a corner or cutting across the lawn.

Dwarf plants may be used in rock gardens, as low hedges, as edging plants along garden walks or in front of flower borders, and to achieve a "naturalistic" effect. Some plants may be placed in a woodland setting; others may be used to stabilize a bank where it has not been possible to establish grass because of large rocks, steep slopes, uneven terrain, or soil erosion. If these shrubs are planted and mulched properly, they will cover the rocks, root wherever their branches touch the soil, and keep the soil from eroding during heavy rains.

Dwarf conifers, combined with deciduous plants, broad-leaved evergreens, perennials, and bulbs, help to set the "scale," establish the basic structure of the garden, and provide visual interest during the winter.

The key word in the small home landscape is "scale." Scale in the public area is the relationship between the mature size of the plants and the size of the house. Small shrubs are usually more appropriate for single-story houses than for larger houses with several stories. Dwarf shrubs are also more aesthetically pleasing and easier to maintain in an attractive form for a longer period of time than the fast-growing shrubs.

Unity is another principle that must be considered. Repetition of similar colors and textures assures harmony, but too much repetition can be monotonous.

Often a small garden can be designed so that it appears larger by employing various techniques in placing plants. An illusion of greater space can be created by placing a few small plants in a strategic location. Coarse-leaved plants in the foreground and finely leaved plants in the background create an illusion of depth in the setting. Carefully chosen dwarf shrubs help to maintain this illusion for a longer period of time than taller growing shrubs because they do not outgrow the space. A vertical garden (vines, espaliered plants, and hanging baskets) against a wall or fence can also increase the illusion of greater space.

A need still exists for quick-growing shrubs and large trees to provide an effect in a short time, especially for the newly constructed house in the subdivision that was a cornfield only a year earlier. But the use of dwarf plants or low shrubs in the home landscape provides permanent interest, beauty, and low maintenance. The most attractive landscape for year-round appearance combines trees, shrubs, and dwarf shrubs.

Dwarf shrubs may be used to stabilize soil on steep banks and above retaining walls.

A foundation planting of large, upright, and spreading needle evergreens will grow out of scale with the house, partially concealing the house and making it seem smaller than it is.

A foundation planting of small and dwarf deciduous and evergreen shrubs remains in scale with the house for an indefinite period of time.

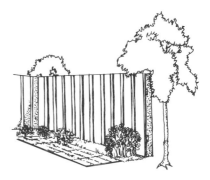

You can create an illusion of space by properly placing small shrubs according to texture and size.

Choosing the Correct Plant for the Site

In selecting a plant for a site, you must first consider the conditions of the site itself: soil characteristics, available sunlight, annual rainfall, location of the site with respect to the house and visual interest, and the desired ultimate height and width of the planting area.

Select plants that will grow well under the conditions of the site. Evaluate each plant for its ornamental characteristics— flowering and fruiting, foliage texture, autumn color, ornamental bark, and growth habit — hardiness, landscape suitability, pest resistance, and ultimate size. Often the homeowner is tempted to buy a small flowering forsythia bush on the nursery lot without realizing that this bush will eventually become 8 to 10 feet high and 8 to 10 feet wide.

It is difficult to state definitely the ultimate height and width for a plant growing in a particular site. There are many complex elements that vary from locale to locale: the severity of winter weather, high summer temperatures, soil characteristics, humidity, amount of rainfall, intensity of sunlight, and the presence of polluting elements.

An arbitrary height of 4 feet was set for most of the plants described in this book. A few plants have been included that may grow higher than 4 feet because of their tolerance to the growing conditions in the Midwest and their value in the landscape. Many taller growing plants can be maintained at a lower height. Even with careful pruning, however, the plants may suffer a loss in the number of flowers and fruits.

Permanent Landscape Containers

The use of permanent landscape containers as a decorative accent is an integral part of the landscape design. These containers should be used in high-interest areas that have solid artificial surfaces, such as patios, decks, roof gardens, paved terraces, and porches.

The site selected for a permanent landscape container should be in a protected area to minimize the effects of rapidly fluctuating summer and winter temperatures. It should also be near a water source.

The plant should be hardy, of specimen quality (with ornamental characteristics that persist throughout the year), and should be known to thrive under the restricting conditions of the landscape container. A woody plant in an aboveground container is subjected to higher summer temperatures, lower winter temperatures, and greater water stress than the same plant in the ground. These conditions can injure or kill the hardiest plant, and plants grown in containers require careful, regular maintenance.

Most container plants should be moved in winter to a protected site to minimize the severity of winds and

sun. If the container is large and heavy, place casters on the bottom so that it can be easily moved from one location to another.

Containers may be purchased in various sizes or homemade. Those with simple lines and earth-tone colors blend well in an informal garden setting. The color should complement other colors on the site. The container should not attract attention to itself but should enhance the plant and the site.

Containers can be constructed of clay, wood, concrete, fiberglass, plastic, or glazed ceramic. To prevent cracking, insulate the sides with 1- to 2-inch-thick sheets of styrofoam to allow for expansion and contraction of the water in the growing medium. Styrofoam also insulates the roots against rapidly fluctuating summer and winter temperatures that can cause root damage.

The depth of the container is important. The container must be sufficiently deep to allow drainage of the soil and expansion of the growing roots. Minimum depths are ½ to 1 foot for flowers, 1½ to 3 feet for large ground covers or dwarf shrubs, and 3 to 5 feet for large shrubs and trees. *The container must have drainage holes in the bottom so that the excess water may drain.* About 5 unobstructed ½-inch holes per square foot are recommended. Too much water remaining around the roots causes them to rot. Raise the plant container slightly above ground level to allow proper air circulation and facilitate drainage.

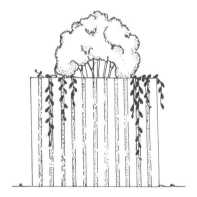

Permanent landscape container (exterior)

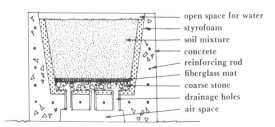

open space for water
styrofoam
soil mixture
concrete
reinforcing rod
fiberglass mat
coarse stone
drainage holes
air space

Permanent landscape container (cross-section)

The soil in the container must drain more rapidly than topsoil. Topsoil alone is not a satisfactory growing medium for plants in containers because it does not have sufficient depth to drain through capillary action (the movement of moisture through the soil from soil particle to particle). A soil mix should provide adequate aeration and retain enough water to grow the plant successfully.

The soil mix usually recommended is 1 part sand, 1 part peat moss or organic matter, and 1 part sterilized soil. Lime and other soil nutrients should be added at this time. The best soil mixture for a particular container depends upon the depth of the container and the plant's requirements. A shallow container requires a coarser textured mix than a deeper one. An acid soil must be provided for those plants that require it.

An organic mulch such as hardwood bark should be applied to the soil surface. The mulch is not only attractive but prevents the topsoil from blowing away and moisture from evaporating too rapidly.

The plants need frequent supplemental watering because they dry out faster than plants in the ground. The frequency of watering depends upon weather conditions, the particular plant, the soil mix, and the design of the container. Plants require more water on sunny, windy days than on cool, cloudy days.

Because water tends to leach out the nutrients, it is necessary to apply fertilizer more frequently to maintain a healthy plant. A complete fertilizer (10-6-4 or 12-12-12) should be applied in small amounts regularly through spring and early summer until the Fourth of July. Fertilizer applied late in the growing season stimulates new growth that is unable to "harden off" before the onset of winter and is susceptible to winter-kill.

Liquid fertilizers need to be applied in smaller amounts than dry fertilizers. Liquid fertilizers are more readily available to the plant, and may "burn" the plant if applied in large amounts. For this reason, *apply liquid fertilizers only as needed*. Follow the instructions on the label carefully. When possible, use slow-release fertilizers in container plantings.

Many container plants should be moved in late autumn to a protected site. These plants become dormant in the winter, and need a cool site such as an unheated porch or garage. If the container is too large to move, you must screen the plant from winter winds and sun. Screening is necessary to protect broad-leaved evergreens from full winter sun after leaf fall from surrounding trees. Bright sun and strong winter winds cause severe moisture loss from the leaves and even kill the plants. A wooden or burlap screen should be loosely constructed around the plant, and left open at the top to provide ventilation. Water the plants thoroughly before the soil freezes.

Hardiness

Hardiness is the ability of a plant to thrive in a particular environment. The hardiness of a plant is affected by the duration and intensity of sunlight, length of growing season, altitude, minimum winter temperatures, amount and timing of rainfall, length and severity of summer drouths, soil characteristics and conditions, proximity to a large body of water, location of the site with reference to a slope, frost occurrence, humidity, and cultural practices.

Plants in their native areas are growing under optimal conditions to meet their needs. The nearer your site approximates native conditions (precipitation, minimum and maximum temperatures, soil characteristics, etc.), the hardier the plant and the better it performs. Even though the garden is within a certain hardiness zone, the "microclimate" that exists on the site of the garden may differ because of structures or plants that modify the temperature, wind, sun, and precipitation on the site. The site may also be influenced by the slope of the land, large paved surfaces, low spots, etc.

"Burning" or browning of evergreen foliage during the winter does not necessarily indicate lack of hardiness. The injury, when confined to one side of the plant, may be the result of exposure to high winds and winter sun. When the ground is frozen, high winds cause the foliage to lose water rapidly. The plant, unable to replace this water with its roots encased in frozen soil, suffers from dessication (drying out). The air temperature surrounding the plant may suddenly drop as the sun goes around a corner, causing winter burn. Protection from sun and wind can reduce dessication and winter burn.

The plant hardiness zone map on page 14 has been adapted from the map issued by the U.S. Department of Agriculture. Each of the 10 zones shown on the map represents an area of winter hardiness based upon average minimum winter temperatures ranging from —50° F. or below in Zone 1 to +30° to 40° F. in Zone 10. The temperatures in adjacent zones become increasingly similar near the common boundary. Within each zone many separate local climates exist that may be warmer or colder than the zone average.

A plant is usually listed in the coldest zone in which it will grow normally. The plant can also be expected to live in a warmer zone if growth conditions (rainfall, soil, summer heat, etc.) are comparable or capable of being made comparable through irrigation, soil correction, wind protection, partial shade, or humidity control. Some plants may be grown in isolated areas north of their designated zone, but may not perform normally or may suffer from winter injury such as dieback or death of the flower buds.

Shaded Sites

Nearly every residential property has some area that receives little or no sun. Shady sites are generally considered problem areas because of the difficulty of establishing and maintaining a high-quality turf, but these sites are excellent for many of the shade-loving dwarf shrubs, as well as colorful bulb, perennial, and annual flowering plants.

There are two kinds of shade: (1) the shade cast by structures; and (2) the shade cast by plants.

The shade cast by a structure is present year-around. It has a "microclimate" different from that in the adjacent area in the sun and is usually cooler.

The shade cast by plants produces various degrees of shade upon the ground, depending upon the density of the foliage and branches. The leaves drop from deciduous plants in the fall, exposing plantings to the winter sun and causing winter burn, especially to the broadleaf evergreens and the *Thuja* (arborvitaes). In addition, dwarf shrubs planted beneath or near large shrubs and trees must compete with the larger plants for water and nutrients.

Collecting Samples for a Soil Test

Before preparing the beds for planting, you should have your soil tested. Soil samples should be taken when the soil temperature is above 50° F., preferably in late October or early November. Collect several soil samples from well-distributed locations in each area in which the planting will take place. The soil must be dry enough so that it does not form a clump when pressed in the hand. Do not take samples after a recent lime or fertilizer application.

Samples may be collected with a soil probe, or by inserting a spade deeply into the ground and taking a vertical core or slice of the soil that is spaded. Discard roots and debris. The vertical core should be about ½ inch thick and 1 inch wide. The depth of the soil sample depends upon the plant material to be established upon the site. The sample should be 3 to 4 inches deep for lawn areas, 6 to 8 inches deep for flower beds and vegetable gardens, and 10 to 12 inches deep for trees and shrubs.

After you have collected all of the samples from one area, air dry the soil and mix thoroughly. Enclose the sample in a sack and pack in a sturdy container. Mail the sample, along with a small fee, to your local county extension adviser, the agronomy department of your state land-grant university, or to an independent soil-testing laboratory. Be sure to provide at least ½ pint of soil per area, along with the intended use of the area (turf, shrub border, etc.), and your name and address.

The test results indicate the amounts of lime and fertilizer that should be applied according to the intended use of the area.

Preparing the Beds

You must prepare the beds carefully so that the soil drains properly and contains the required nutrients for establishing the plants quickly. Stake out the dimensions of the bed on the ground, and hand spade the soil as deeply as possible, preferably 12 inches or more.

If you use a rototiller, you must hand spade near the house to avoid damage to the house or rototiller. Remove any debris found in the soil. Often construction materials are buried just beneath the ground surface, including mortar or plasterboard that contains large amounts of lime, raising the pH of the surrounding soil.

If there is a shallow topsoil and a heavy clay subsoil, the topsoil should be set aside and the clay soil excavated and discarded. Organic matter or peat moss can then be incorporated with the topsoil to replace the clay soil that was removed.

Disturbing the soil profile also affects the percolation (excess water flowing downward through the soil). It is necessary to supply abundant amounts of organic matter and humus (peat moss, leaf mold, or compost) to obtain adequate air space and water penetration.

Organic materials will allow water to percolate freely down through the soil.

Although it is preferable to use organic matter to provide drainage, sand can be used for this purpose. To be effective, the sand must constitute 50 percent or more of the total soil mass; otherwise the sand adds solids to the soil.

If the site still does not drain properly, place drain tiles in the bed about 18 inches below the ground level. Add a shallow layer of gravel over the tile. The drain tile can carry the water off to a catch basin or drainage ditch. Gravel alone should *not* be placed in the bottom of the planting hole. Gravel serves as an air bubble or cistern to collect water.

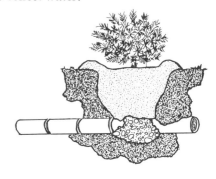

Use drainage tile to eliminate excess moisture. ***Do not use gravel alone in the bottom of the planting hole.***

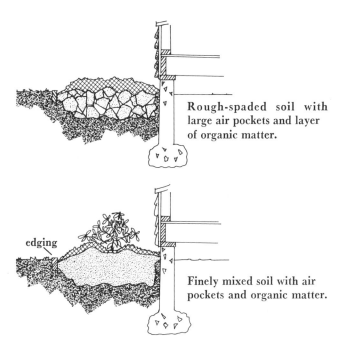

Rough-spaded soil with large air pockets and layer of organic matter.

edging

Finely mixed soil with air pockets and organic matter.

To prepare a planting bed, spade the soil to a depth of 12 to 14 inches and add a layer of organic matter (top). Continue mixing the soil and organic matter until the planting bed is "fluffy" and well drained (bottom).

If the results of the soil test indicated that fertilizer or lime should be added, incorporate these materials when preparing the bed. Work the soil until all the components are thoroughly mixed. Prepare the bed a considerable time before planting so that it has time to settle. A minimum of several weeks is necessary, but allowing the bed to settle over the winter is preferable.

It is strongly recommended that the plants be placed in beds instead of scattered around the lawn ("shot-gun" effect). Install an edging to make a sharp delineation between the bed area and the lawn area. This edging makes it easier to maintain a clean separation between the two areas. It may be constructed of Ryerson steel, extruded aluminum, pre-servative-treated wood, brick, or railroad ties.

Planting

Plant shrubs as quickly after purchase as possible. If you cannot plant for some time, place the shrubs on a protected site and check daily to see if additional water is necessary. It is usually best to transplant in the late afternoon or on a cloudy day. The plants need protection from the hot sun and sweeping winds to prevent drying out, and the roots and soil ball must be kept moist.

When planting in a newly prepared bed, dig the hole slightly deeper and slightly wider than the size of the root ball. In an established bed, dig the hole much larger and discard some of the soil. Add peat moss,

compost, or leaf mold and mix with the soil. Firm the soil at the bottom of the hole so that the plant does not settle after it is placed in the hole and watered.

Place the shrub in the hole at precisely the same depth that it was growing previously. Orient the plant so that its best side is facing the direction from which it will be viewed. If you purchased a **bare-root** plant, the roots were packed in a moist medium (usually wood shavings or sphagnum moss) and placed in a plastic package. Remove the package and examine the roots. Cut off any broken roots and branches. Soak the roots in water for 24 hours before planting.

Dig a hole large enough to accommodate the roots without crowding them. Build up a mound of soil in the bottom of the hole and spread the roots out over the mound. The hole should be **backfilled** quickly so that the roots do not dry out.

There are two recommended methods of backfilling a hole. In the first method, the dry soil is replaced in the hole and firmed around the roots. When the hole has been filled in, the backfilled soil is thoroughly saturated with water. In the second method, soil and water are added to the hole at the same time to form a "mud slurry." This slurry removes all air pockets around and under the root ball and allows you to observe the percolation of the soil (how fast the water drains from the hole). The root ball may be easily adjusted if it is too deep or the plant is tilted. If the water does not percolate properly, you may need to install drainage tile.

If the plant you purchased is **balled-and-burlapped,** dig the hole somewhat larger than the size of the root ball. Without removing the twine that keeps the root ball intact, place the root ball in the hole and position it so that it is sitting at the proper height and its best side is oriented toward the area from which the plant will be viewed. The root ball must be kept intact. If it breaks, the small feeder roots also break, resulting in severe injury or death to the plant.

Once the plant is in proper position, you must remove the twine and burlap from the trunk to prevent the twine from girdling the growing plant and the burlap from drying out the root ball. If the burlap is brown, it is untreated. Untreated burlap will quickly decompose, and can be stuffed back in the hole. If the burlap is green, it has been treated against decay, and must be completely removed from the hole. If the shrub is planted with the burlap and twine intact, the twine, which does not decay, restricts the roots from spreading into the adjacent soil.

If you purchased a shrub in a **container** (tar paper, paper mâché, plastic, metal, etc.), you *must* remove the container before planting. Examine the root system. If the plant has been growing in the container for a year or longer, the roots will encircle the root ball. These roots should be straightened out or cut off.

Planting a shrub in a fibrous container with a portion of the rim extending above the soil may be fatal to the shrub. The fibrous material of the container attracts the water from the root ball and allows it to evaporate into the air. The rim also prevents water from entering the pot when supplemental water is applied. As a result, conditions inside the container may be drouthy, while those immediately surrounding the container may be quite moist.

Frequently there is an **interface** problem. This condition exists when the soil around the roots is of a different type from the soil on the site. The roots do not grow into the adjacent soil, and the plant does not become firmly established on the site. Mixing a portion of the two soils helps to alleviate this problem.

Build a saucer of soil around the planting hole on the surface of the ground. At least for the first growing season, the shrub will need supplemental watering. The saucer prevents the water from running off and directs it to the roots.

When the plant is in the ground and the soil has been replaced around the roots, apply a water-soluble starter fertilizer (such as 0-45-0 or 10-50-17) during the first watering. A starter fertilizer (one that is high in phosphorus) is essential to root establishment.

If part of the roots were lost in transplanting, selectively prune the aboveground portion of the plant to restore a balance between the stems and the roots. This pruning allows the plant to become established more quickly. Newly planted shrubs should also be mulched (see **Mulching** below).

Mulching

Most plants benefit from an organic mulch applied to the soil surface. A mulch serves the following purposes:

1. Keeps the soil moist and cool.
2. Prohibits the surface of the soil from drying.
3. Reduces rapid fluctuations of soil temperatures.
4. Inhibits weed-seed germination, reducing competition from weeds for moisture and nutrients.
5. Stops soil crusting or caking under the force of irrigation or rain.
6. Prevents soot and other finely textured airborne particles from sealing the soil surface.
7. Provides acid and nutrients as it decomposes.
8. Eliminates the need for deep cultivation that severs the surface roots, reducing plant growth.

Suitable organic mulches include hardwood bark, composted oak leaves, composted organic matter, pine needles, and mushroom compost. Peat moss is not suitable as a mulch. It is difficult to wet — and once it

dries, it blows away. Uncomposted material should not be used because it ties up the nitrogen-fixing bacteria in the initial stage of decomposition.

The depth of the mulch depends upon the material used. It should be deep enough to prevent weeds from growing through it and yet allow air and light rain to penetrate it, and should be maintained throughout the year. Additional materials should be applied whenever the mulch begins to break down. Adding nitrogen when the mulch is applied assures an adequate supply of nitrogen for the plant.

Some gardeners use black plastic instead of an organic mulch to reduce the number of weeds. Black plastic is not recommended for ornamental plantings because the soil beneath the plastic collects moisture that does not evaporate. As a result, the roots become waterlogged and rot.

Some gardeners place rocks on the surface of the black plastic. The plastic will be ripped easily unless it is laid on a cushion of sand and covered with rounded rocks. When the plastic is ripped, sunlight penetrates the soil, causing weed seed to germinate and defeating the purpose for which the plastic was used. If calcium-bearing stone is used as a mulch, the calcium alters the pH of the site.

Watering

During the first one or two growing seasons, the plant will need about 1 inch of water once or twice a week, depending upon the temperature and amount of rainfall. Maintain the mound or saucer of soil around the base of each plant to direct the water to the roots. You can determine the amount of water applied during irrigation by placing a shallow container with straight sides beneath the sprinkler and measuring the amount of water it collects.

Supplemental water should be applied in early morning so that the plant can dry off during the day. Water applied in late afternoon or in the evening remains on the plant. The "wet" condition of the plant and the "cool" temperatures of the evening promote fungal disease.

In very hot weather, the leaf surfaces of the plant may be cooled by a spray of water. The water can be applied when the plant is in full sun without danger of the leaves "burning."

Before the ground freezes in late fall, give the plants a thorough soaking, especially those that retain their leaves during the winter months. These plants continue to **transpire** (give off water through the leaves) during the winter when the temperature is above freezing. They cannot replace this water because their roots are encased in frozen ground.

Pruning

If you considered the ultimate height and width of a dwarf plant before purchasing it, you should not need to trim the plant because it has grown too large for the site. Usually the only pruning necessary is (1) to cut out dead, broken, and insect- or disease-infested wood; (2) to remove branches that rub against each other and cause wounds, or branches that produce an asymmetrical habit; and (3) to compensate for the loss of roots (especially in bare-root plants) when the plant was dug.

Multistemmed shrubs may be pruned by the **renewal method.** Remove a number of old stems each spring by pruning them back to 3 or 4 inches above the ground. Renewal pruning opens up the plant, allowing sunlight to enter, promotes new growth, maintains the size of the plant, and encourages flowering and fruiting.

When multistemmed plants become too large or contain many dead branches, the plants may be pruned by the **rejuvenation method.** Every 2 or 3 years in early spring, prune the plants to 3 to 4 inches above the ground (for example, *Spiraea* × *bumalda* cutivars and *Deutzia gracilis*).

Single-stemmed plants should be pruned by the **heading-back method.** Prune the unwanted branches on an angle at the crotch of a main limb or ¼ inch above a bud. Do not leave a stub. A stub is not only unsightly, but the wood dies back to the nearest bud or growing point, becoming an avenue of entry for insect and diseases into the plant.

Study the plant and choose the branches that you are going to remove. Do not "behead" the plant or shear it into an unnatural, artificial shape. The new growth is unattractive, and produces a leggy, bushy-topped plant. Always prune to maintain the natural growth habit of the plant.

Use a sharp pair of hand pruners to make a clean cut. A clean cut heals faster and reduces the possibility of insects and diseases entering the plant. Hand pruners with two cutting edges make a cleaner cut than those with one blunt and one bypass cutting edge. Be sure to disinfect your tools with alcohol after each cut on insect- or disease-infested wood.

You must know whether the plant flowers on new growth produced in the current season or on wood produced the preceding season. If the plant flowers on new growth, prune in early spring before the new growth starts; if the plant flowers on wood produced the preceding year, prune the plant immediately after it has flowered. For many plants, such as *Rhododendron,* removing the flowers before the seeds develop usually results in a larger flower display the following spring. The nutrients that would have produced the fruits are diverted into setting flower buds for the next season.

Fertilizing

One of the valuable characteristics of dwarf plants is their slow growth rate. Fertilizer aids growth when applied to dwarf plants in early spring. Well-rotted manure or compost placed around the plants slowly releases nutrients and is quite satisfactory. Chemical fertilizers may also be used.

Apply chemical fertilizers strictly according to the directions on the label. Applying too much fertilizer or fertilizing after June first can cause dwarf plants to produce new growth that does not have time to "harden off" before the onset of winter and is subject to winter damage.

For bare-root plants or plants that need to be established quickly, use a water-soluble starter fertilizer (0-45-0 or 10-50-17). These fertilizers are high in phosphorus, and phosphorus is essential to establishing the roots rapidly.

The easiest method for applying fertilizer is to "broadcast" it (scatter it evenly) on top of the soil. Apply when the foliage is dry so that the fertilizer does not stick to the leaves and cause burning. Water immediately to wash fertilizer from the leaves and into the soil.

Apply liquid fertilizers in smaller amounts than dry fertilizers. Liquid fertilizers are more readily available to the plant, and may "burn" the plant if applied in large amounts.

Winter Protection

Winter protection begins with the selection of plants that are winter hardy for a particular area. There are certain cultural practices that will improve the over-wintering of plants.

Do not prune after the Fourth of July or fertilize after June first. Late fertilization and pruning stimulate new growth that cannot "harden off" before the onset of winter and is subject to winter damage.

Any insect- or disease-infested wood should be removed as soon as possible. The infestation weakens the plant so that it is susceptible to winter injury.

The broad-leaved evergreens and conifers should be watered thoroughly in late fall. Much winter injury is the result of desiccation (drying out). These plants are unable to absorb additional water to replace the water lost during transpiration (evaporation of water through the leaves) because the roots are in frozen ground and are not functional.

The water loss is higher when the plants are located where winter winds are high and the winter sun is bright and warm. The roots absorb soil moisture as long as it is available. The plant continues to transpire even when water is not available because of drouthy or frozen soil conditions. Because the roots are unable to replace the water lost through the leaves, water is taken from the living cells. When the plant becomes too dried out, the cells die, resulting in the death of the evergreen foliage.

Broad-leaved evergreens need protection from winter sun and winds. This protection may be provided by the site itself or by placing the plants in front of a windbreak. If a windbreak has not been established, the same effect can be created by sticking pine branches in the ground around the windward side of the plant.

Antitranspirants are often used to prevent rapid loss of moisture through the leaves of broad-leaved evergreens or conifers. Wax or a waxlike material (latex, acrylic, etc.) is sprayed on the leaf surfaces to slow transpiration, especially in sunny or windy sites. The material slows transpiration by sealing the leaf surfaces and closing the stomates. Antitranspirants are costly, often difficult to apply, and may burn the foliage if applied improperly. In addition, the effects of the application may not last throughout the winter. Antitranspirants should be used in combination with proper watering and mulching practices.

Alternate freezing and thawing of the soil, especially in early spring, can force young or shallow-rooted plants to "heave" out of the soil, exposing their roots. If the roots dry out, the plant will die unless they are immediately recovered with soil. To reduce damage from heaving, apply 3 to 4 inches of mulch in late fall. Mulch will also keep the soil warm in the fall and cool later in the spring.

Propagation

Most of the plants described in this book are cultivars, varieties, or clones that must be propagated by asexual means (cuttings, grafting, layering, and division) to retain the identical characteristics of the parent plant. Relatively few of the plants may be propagated by seed (sexual) propagation, with the resultant seedlings identical with the parent plants. Only those plants that are the straight species should be propagated by seeds.

Most of the deciduous and broad-leaved evergreens may be easily propagated by softwood cuttings collected in late spring or early summer. Rooting is enhanced when a rooting hormone is applied to the cutting. Several commercial products are available.

Conifers root most satisfactorily when the cuttings are collected in late fall or early winter after one or more hard frosts. A rooting hormone should be applied. Some conifers do not successfully root from cuttings. *Pinus* (pine), *Pseudotsuga* (hemlock), and some *Picea* (spruce) must be grafted.

Nomenclature

The botanical name is the internationally recognized name for a particular plant. Its stem is usually Latin, Greek, or a proper name or descriptive term, and has a Latinized ending. The botanical name consists of two names: the first identifies the **genus,** and the second (**specific epithet**) identifies a particular member of the genus. Together the genus and specific epithet constitute the name of the **species.** The first letter of the genus name is always capitalized, and the specific epithet is commonly written in lower case letters. The species name is underlined or italicized (for example, *Cotoneaster horizontalis*).

The **species** (plural also **species**) is the basic unit in a classification system whose members are structurally similar, have common ancestors, and maintain their characteristic features in nature through innumerable generations.

The **genus** (plural **genera**) may be defined as a more or less closely related and definable group of plants comprising one or more species. The unifying characteristic of a genus is a similarity of flowers and fruits. A group of closely related genera is called a **family.** The botanical name of the family is usually recognizable by its — acaea ending. The stem of the name is the name of one of the genera within the family. For example, *Buxacaea* is the family name in which *Buxus* (Box) is a genus.

A **variety** is a subdivision of a species, and exhibits various inheritable morphological characteristics (form and structure) that are perpetuated through both sexual and asexual propagation. A variety is designated by a trinomial (three names). The varietal term is written in lower case and underlined or italicized. It is sometimes written with the abbreviation **var.** placed between the specific epithet and the variety terms (for example, *Juniperus chinensis sargentii* or *Juniperus chinensis* var. *sargentii*).

A **cultivar** (the term is a contraction of "cultivated variety") is a group of plants within a particular species that is distinguished by one or more characteristics (morphological, physiological, chemical, etc.), and that, when reproduced sexually or asexually, retains these characteristics. The cultivar term may be one to three names. Each name in the term begins with a capital letter. The term is commonly written inside single quotation marks (as in this book), but it may be preceded by the abbreviation **cv.,** and is not underlined or italicized (for example, *Berberis thunbergii* 'Crimson Pygmy' or *Berberis thunbergii* cv. Crimson Pygmy). When cultivars are of hybrid or unknown cultivars, they may sometimes be written without a specific epithet (for example, *Philadelphus* 'Silver Showers').

A **clone** (or **clon**) is a group of plants that originated from a single plant, and have been propagated by asexual means (taking cuttings, grafting, dividing, and budding and layering) to maintain the exact characteristics of the parent plant.

The name of a hybrid is preceded by a multiplication sign ($\times$) between the generic name and the specific epithet. The names of the parents are listed with the multiplication sign between them. For example, *Spiraea* $\times$ *bumalda* is a hybrid of *Spiraea albiflora* $\times$ *Spiraea japonica*. In the case of *Spiraea* $\times$ *bumalda* 'Anthony Waterer', 'Anthony Waterer' is a cultivar of the hybrid plant.

Each plant that has been recognized and described has only one valid name — its botanical name (consisting of the name of the genus and the specific epithet). This binominal system of nomenclature was created by Carolus Linnaeus (1707-1778) in his book *Species Plantarum* (1753). The nomenclature is controlled by the International Association for Plant Taxonomy, which issues an *International Code of Botanical Nomenclature* that is strictly adhered to throughout the world. The *International Code of Nomenclature for Cultivated Plants,* which governs the rules for naming cultivars, is issued by the International Union of Botanical Sciences. Both of these Codes are revised periodically.

The botanical name for each of the plants described in this book appears on the upper left of the page, followed by the family name and the hardiness zone or zones (see page 7) in which the plant can be successfully grown. The common name or names appear on the upper right of the page, followed, in some cases, by the "obsolete" botanical name or names under which the plant may be listed by certain nurseries. The nomenclature, especially in the conifers, can become confusing in attempting to identify a particular plant. For this reason, you should always use the botanical name when ordering a plant. Because common names are not governed by any formal code of nomenclature, and because there are frequently many common names for one species (some of which are obsolete), the use of a common name can be confusing and lead to mistaken identities.

For information about nurseries and other sources for the plants described in this book, consult your county Extension Service office or the horticulture department of your state land-grant university.

Typical Entry

(1) *Arctostaphylos uva-ursi*

---

(2) *Ericaceae* (Heath family)

(3) Zone 2

(4) Bearberry, Kinnikinick, Mealberry, Mountain Box

(5) May also be listed as *Arbutus uva-ursi*

1. botanical name
2. family name
3. hardiness zone

4. common names
5. obsolete botanical name

Hardiness Zone Map

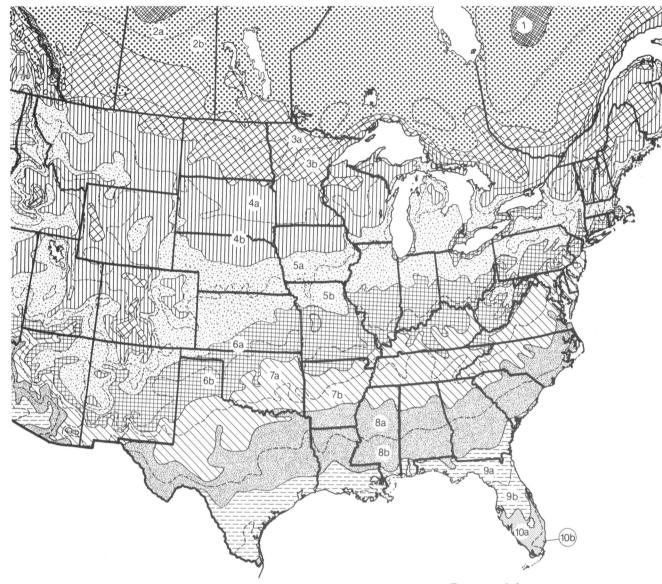

Each zone of the map has been subdivided into 5-degree increments. The portion above the dotted line (designated by the letter "a") represents the colder section of the zone; the portion below the dotted line ("b") represents the warmer section.

Adapted from U.S. Department of Agriculture plant hardiness zone map of the United States.

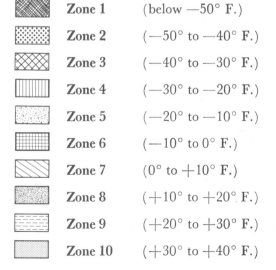

**Range of Average
Annual Minimum Temperatures**

	Zone 1	(below —50° F.)
	Zone 2	(—50° to —40° F.)
	Zone 3	(—40° to —30° F.)
	Zone 4	(—30° to —20° F.)
	Zone 5	(—20° to —10° F.)
	Zone 6	(—10° to 0° F.)
	Zone 7	(0° to +10° F.)
	Zone 8	(+10° to +20° F.)
	Zone 9	(+20° to +30° F.)
	Zone 10	(+30° to +40° F.)

Plant Descriptions

Deciduous Plants

Berberidaceae (Barberry family)

Zone 6

Crimson Pygmy Japanese Barberry

May also be listed as
Berberis thunbergii 'Crimson Pygmy'

leaves and fruit   flower and thorn

Berberis thunbergii 'Atropurpurea Nana' is a round, compacted dwarf shrub that usually grows 2 to 3 feet high and 4 feet wide. Growth rate is slow. Texture is medium.

The leaves are deciduous, alternate, simple, entire, and about ½ to ¾ inch long. They are a deep crimson with a brownish tinge when grown in full sun, and a greenish red if grown in partial shade. The color is retained throughout the growing season. The newer foliage appears as a brighter red. A single spine usually grows from each node, with a pair of appendages at the basal end of the spine.

The inner wood of the plant is yellow.

The ⅜-inch-long, campanulate (bell-shaped) flowers have a waxlike beauty, and vary in color from pale yellow to orange or red. They are borne singly or in clusters in great profusion in mid-May.

The red, oval-shaped, ¼-inch-long berries are not as numerous as the berries of *Berberis thunbergii*. The fruits ripen in late June. They are not eaten by birds, and persist throughout the winter.

Berberis thunbergii 'Atropurpurea Nana' is a very adaptable plant that tolerates a wide range of conditions. Full sun is necessary to develop the brightest crimson-colored foliage. The plant is easy to move. It is brittle, and can be easily broken when transplanted or after it has become established. Any soil that does not waterlog is satisfactory. To prune this single-stem plant, use the "heading back" principle. The plant is not seriously affected by insects or diseases.

This barberry may be used as a low hedge (plants spaced 1 to 2 feet apart) in a small enclosure near the patio or for emphasis inside a bed, *provided that the leaf color is not objectionable*. It may also be used in the foundation planting, shrub border, a mass planting, rock garden, a permanent landscape container, as an edging, and as a specimen plant.

Berberis thunbergii 'Atropurpurea Nana' is easily propagated from softwood cuttings taken in late spring or early summer.

This plant has been sold under several names, including 'Little Gem', 'Little Favorite', and 'Little Beauty'. Other cultivars of *Berberis thunbergii* are 'Rose Glow' (leaves are mottled green and white with rose-red cast; new growth is quite red) and 'Kobold' (dwarf, bright-green foliage).

Rosaceae (Rose family)

Zone 4

Japanese Flowering Quince

May also be listed as
Cydonia japonica

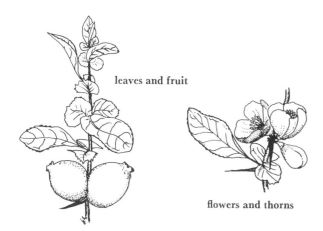

leaves and fruit

flowers and thorns

Chaenomeles japonica is a low, densely spreading shrub that grows 3 to 4 feet high and 4 feet or more wide. Growth rate is fast. Texture is medium in winter but coarse in summer.

The branches bear long, sharply pointed spines at the tip of the branches and in the leaf axils. The twigs are rough and hairy, with minute warts.

The handsome leaves are deciduous, alternate, simple, toothed, leathery, oval-shaped, and 1 to 2 inches long. They bear large stipules (a pair of leafy appendages at the basal end of the petiole or leafstalk), and taper at the base to a short stalk. The leaves are slightly brownish as they open, becoming dark, glossy green in summer. Fall color is green to brownish.

The showy flowers are orange-red, single, round, and 1¼ inches in diameter. They are borne abundantly from the joints of year-old wood in early May before the leaves appear. The stems may be collected in midwinter and encouraged to flower when placed in a warm room. The plant may attempt to flower in the autumn. Early freezes will kill the swollen or partly expanded flower buds.

The pleasantly scented fruit is a yellow pome, 1½ inches in diameter, with a red blotch on the side exposed to the sun. The fruit ripens in late summer. It makes an excellent jelly but is unpalatable when fresh. This plant is often self-sterile (cannot adequately fertilize itself), and sets little or no fruit, especially when grown singly.

Chaenomeles japonica transplants easily and requires little care. It tolerates any good garden soil, but grows best in a well-drained, loamy soil. Full sun is required to promote abundant flowering. *Chaenomeles* occasionally needs renewal pruning. Since the flowers are borne on year-old wood, prune immediately after flowering.

This plant has sparse foliage that defoliates in hot weather because of fungus diseases. It is not seriously affected by insects or other diseases.

Chaenomeles japonica may be used in the foundation planting, shrub border, or as a hedge (plants spaced 2 feet apart). It should not be used where the thorns could create a problem to pedestrians or children. The plant can become unsightly, especially if it is placed as an important focal point in the home landscape, because it tends to collect windblown trash that is difficult to remove.

Propagation is by seed, softwood cuttings of new growth in late spring or early summer, and by transplanting the rooted underground offshoots (suckers).

The cultivar *Chaenomeles* $\times$ *superba* 'Boule de Feu' has semidouble red flowers.

Chaenomeles japonica is native to Japan. It was introduced in 1874.

For a color illustration of *Chaenomeles japonica*, see page 138.

Myricaceae (Bayberry family)   Sweetfern

Zone 3

leaves and flower

Comptonia peregrina is a graceful, broad, spreading shrub with erect branches that form a flat-topped or rounded outline. This plant grows 4 feet high, and can spread 4 to 8 feet. Growth rate is slow to medium. Texture is medium.

The fragrant leaves are deciduous, alternate, simple, lobed, 2 to 4½ inches long and ⅔ inch wide, pubescent (hairy), and resemble fern fronds. They emerge pale green, turning dark green with age. Autumn coloration is not ornamental.

The flowers are not conspicuous. They are borne in yellow-green catkins (pendulous, scaly spikes) in April and early May.

The fruit is an olive-brown nutlet, ⅓ inch long, and is not ornamental.

Comptonia peregrina grows in acid, peaty or sandy soil in full sun or partial shade. This plant affixes nitrogen, allowing it to adapt to poor soils. It is very difficult to transplant and establish because it has a shallow, fibrous root system, and should be purchased as a container-grown plant. It is not seriously affected by insects or diseases.

Comptonia peregrina is best used for "naturalizing" in a wild garden or on a bank where the soil is infertile.

This plant is difficult to propagate. It can be rooted with cuttings taken from juvenile wood in late winter or early spring before growth starts, dipped in a hormone rooting compound, and placed under mist. It is usually propagated by root cuttings.

Comptonia peregrina is related to *Myrica* (Bayberry), and is native to Nova Scotia, North Carolina, Indiana, and Michigan.

Comptonia peregrina var. *asplenifolia* has smaller leaves and less pubescence than *Comptonia peregrina*. Under its obsolete name, *Comptonia asplenifolia*, it is more frequently listed by nurseries than *Comptonia peregrina*.

Cornaceae (Dogwood family)

Zone 4

Kelsey Red-Osier Dogwood

May also be listed as
Cornus sericea 'Kelseyi'

leaves and flower head

Cornus stolonifera 'Kelseyi' is a neat, much-branched, round, compact shrub that grows 1½ to 2½ feet high and 2 feet wide. Growth rate is medium. Texture is coarse.

The leaves are deciduous, opposite, simple, entire, oblong, and medium green on the upper sides and lighter green on the undersides. The plant is covered with dense foliage that has no spectacular autumn color in the Midwest. In warmer areas, autumn color is brownish maroon.

Some of the new stems are red, although they are less colorful than the species. The pith (the soft material in the center of the stem) is white.

The dull-white flowers are rarely borne in flat-topped cymes (1½ to 2 inches in diameter) in late May to early June.

The seldom-borne fruits are white, globose drupes (stone fruits). They are often not visible because the weak branches tend to lean over.

Cornus stolonifera 'Kelseyi' can be grown in sun or shade. This plant thrives in moist soils but will grow in dryer soils. It can be cut back to the main stem to promote new growth of brighter colored stems. If the plant is multistemmed, it can be cut back rather severely; if it is single-stemmed, it should be "headed back." The plant should be pruned in the spring before new growth occurs. Leaf blight, a fungus disease, can be a serious problem in areas with poor air movement and water drainage.

Cornus stolonifera 'Kelseyi' may be used in the foundation planting, shrub border, dwarf hedge (plants spaced 1 to 1½ feet apart), or as a ground cover.

Propagation is usually with softwood cuttings taken in late spring or early summer.

Rosaceae (Rose family)

Rockspray, Rock Cotoneaster

Zone 5b

stem and leaves flowers fruit

Cotoneaster horizontalis is grown more for its red fruits and red autumn color than for its flowers. The shrub has a stiff, dense, horizontal, almost prostrate habit. Its ultimate size ranges from 2 to 3 feet high to 5 to 8 feet wide. Growth rate is medium. Texture is medium.

One of the outstanding characteristics of this plant is its beautifully horizontal branching habit; the branches form layered tiers in a fishbone pattern. This pattern becomes even more evident when the plant is defoliated.

The glossy, dark-green leaves are deciduous, alternate, simple, entire, flat, ½ inch long, and roundish or broadly oval. The leaves become a brilliant red in the North in autumn but drop in the South while they are still practically evergreen.

The pink flowers are perfect, round, ¼ inch in diameter, and are borne singly or in pairs in May or June on short, leafy twigs of new wood.

The fruit is a decorative, bright red pome less than ¼ inch wide that persists from late August through October.

Cotoneaster horizontalis requires sun or partial shade in a rich, loamy, well-drained soil. Because it has a sparse, stringy root system, it is difficult to transplant. The plant should be purchased balled-and-burlapped or container-grown, and can be planted in the spring or fall. Pruning should be kept to a minimum because it destroys the beautiful branching habit and promotes the growth and spread of disease within a single plant and from a diseased plant to a healthy one. Many insects and diseases have been reported on *Cotoneaster* plantings. Fire blight, a bacterial disease, can be especially damaging to plantings in the Midwest. Although the plant does not collect as much windblown trash and debris as the taller, upright cotoneasters, it is nevertheless difficult to rake or clean out.

Cotoneaster horizontalis is one of the loveliest species of the large *Rosaceae* family. It is one of the most widely grown and perhaps the best of the low-growing types. It can be used as a specimen plant, at the top of a retaining wall, espaliered against a wall, or in a shrub border, foundation planting, mass planting, or permanent landscape container. Because the effect of its branching habit is diminished if the plant is severely pruned, *Cotoneaster horizontalis* needs space to grow and develop. It can be displayed to best effect in a rock garden or between flagstones where no other plant material can grow through it.

The native habitat for *Cotoneaster horizontalis* is western China. Seed was collected by a missionary named Père David about 1870. The plant was put into the trade in France in 1885.

Cultivars include "Variegata' (leaves with white margins, not as vigorous in growth as the species); 'Little Gem' (a handsome dwarf, mounded, slow-growing); and 'Tom Thumb' (a dwarf similar to 'Little Gem'). *Cotoneaster horizontalis* var. *perpusilla* is more diminutive than the species, with more small branches and larger berries.

Softwood cuttings collected in June will root readily.

For a color illustration of *Cotoneaster horizontalis*, see page 138.

Fabaceae (Legume family)   Prostrate Broom

Zone 6

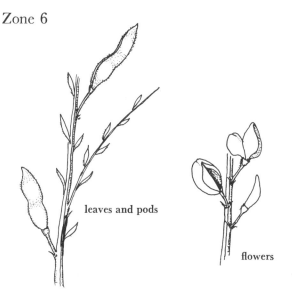

leaves and pods

flowers

Cytisus decumbens is the most prostrate species of the genus in cultivation. It lies flat on the ground and increases in height by laying down additional growths on the older branches, forming a thick, tangled mat. The plant increases equally on all sides and grows about 8 inches high. Growth rate is slow. Texture is fine.

The leaves are deciduous, simple, alternate, stalkless, ¼ to ¾ inch long and ⅛ to 1/16 inch across, and pubescent (hairy), especially on the underside.

The stems remain green throughout the winter. They are 5-angled and sparsely hairy, and are attractive in the winter landscape.

The bright yellow flowers are typical pealike flowers of the *Fabaceae* family. They are ½ to ⅝ inch long, and are borne 1 to 3 in a cluster from the joints of the preceding summer's growth. The flowers are produced most abundantly in May, and then taper off in early August.

The fruit is a hairy pod, ¾ to 1 inch long, and is not showy.

Cytisus decumbens grows best in a sunny exposure and an acid, well-drained, or drouthy soil. It often dies back to the ground during a severe winter, and grows again from the roots the following spring. Because large plants are difficult to move, *Cytisus decumbens* is best purchased as a container-grown plant and placed immediately in its permanent site. The plant is a legume, and nitrogen-bearing nodules form on its roots and enrich the soil. It is not seriously affected by insects or diseases.

Do not cultivate around the plant after it is established. If it is necessary to prune because of winter injury (twig dieback), prune lightly immediately after flowering.

This excellent dwarf can be used in the rock garden or foundation planting as a ground cover.

Genista (page 31) is often mistakenly referred to as "broom." This term should only be applied to the plants in the *Cytisus* genus.

Propagation may be by seed or by cuttings taken in June or early July.

The native habitat of this plant is southern Europe from France to Albania and Montenegro. It was introduced in 1775.

Cytisus procumbens is similar to *Cytisus decumbens* except that it grows to 2½ feet high and several feet wide.

For a color illustration of *Cytisus decumbens,* see page 138.

Thymelaeaceae (Mezereum family)   Somerset Burkwood Daphne

Zone 4

leaves and flower cluster

Daphne × burkwoodii 'Somerset' has a **rounded,** dense, upright habit, growing to an ultimate size of 4 feet high and 6 feet wide. Growth rate is slow. Texture is fine.

The semievergreen leaves are alternate, simple, entire, and 1¼ inches long and ¼ inch wide. They are dark blue-green, narrowly oblong, and have no autumn color.

The pale pinkish-white, fragrant flowers are ⅜ inch wide, tubular-shaped, and 4-lobed. They are borne in dense terminal umbels, 1½ to 2 inches in diameter, and are surrounded by foliage in May and early June.

The fruits are red berries, approximately ⅓ inch wide, that ripen in the fall.

Daphne × burkwoodii 'Somerset' was introduced by the original Wayside Gardens, Mentor, Ohio, in the late 1930's.

For a general discussion of **Daphne,** see page 27.

Thymelaeaceae (Mezereum family)   Rose Daphne, Garland Flower

Zone 6

leaves and flower cluster

Daphne cneorum is a low-spreading shrub with long, trailing branches that form dense mats. It usually grows less than 1 foot high and up to 3 feet wide. Growth rate is slow. Texture is medium-fine in all seasons.

The gray-green leaves are alternate, simple, entire, narrow, 1 inch long and ⅛ to ⅓ inch wide, and dark green on the upper sides and grayish on the undersides. They are more persistent in the southern portion of the Midwest than in the northern. The leaves have no autumn color.

The extremely fragrant, bright rosy pink flowers are ⅖ inch wide, tubular-shaped, and 4-lobed. They are abundantly borne in 6 to 8 flowered umbels through April and May, hiding the foliage. With proper care, the plant will flower sporadically throughout the summer and into September.

The fruit is a yellow-brown berry that ripens in the fall.

Daphne cneorum is a native of central and southern Europe from Spain to southwestern Russia. It was introduced about 1752.

For a color illustration of **Daphne cneorum,** see page 138.

For a general discussion of **Daphne,** see page 27.

Thymelaeaceae (Mezereum family)   Giraldi Daphne

Zone 4

leaves and flower cluster   fruit

Daphne giraldii is an erect shrub about 2 to 3 feet high and 4 feet wide. Growth rate is slow. Texture is fine.

The leaves are deciduous, alternate, simple, entire, stalkless, 1½ to 3 inches long, and ¼ to ⅝ inch wide. They are dark blue-green on the upper sides and glaucous (covered with a grayish powder) on the undersides. This *Daphne* also has no fall color.

The small, slightly fragrant, golden-yellow flowers are 4-lobed, tubular-shaped, and are borne in 4 to 8 flowered umbels that terminate the leafy, young shoots. The plants flower in late May.

The fruits are scarlet, egg-shaped berries approximately ¼ inch long that ripen in July.

Daphne giraldii, one of the hardiest of the genus, is native to northwestern China. The plant was discovered by Père Giraldi in 1894, and introduced by W. Purdom in 1911. This *Daphne* is especially valued for its flowers.

General Discussion of *Daphne*

Daphnes are particular as to their culture. They grow best in slight shade. The soil must be well drained, cool and moist, with a pH range of 5.0 to 7.0. An organic mulch should be used around the plant to create cool, moist conditions in the root zone.

Daphne should be purchased as a balled-and-burlapped or container-grown plant that can be transplanted in early spring so that it has the entire summer to become established before going dormant in the winter. Once established, the plant should be left in the site permanently because it does not tolerate transplanting.

Although *Daphne* rarely needs pruning, it may be pruned annually after flowering. *Daphne cneorum* and *Daphne giraldii* need winter protection (such as a covering of pine boughs) in Zone 6 to insure their survival.

The berries of the daphnes are poisonous, and should not be eaten by children or animals.

Daphne may be used in the foundation planting, rock garden, in front of a shrub border, on top of a wall, or as a ground cover or specimen plant.

Softwood, hardwood, and root cuttings may be taken in the summer and fall.

Saxifragaceae (Saxifrage family)   Slender Deutzia

Zone 5

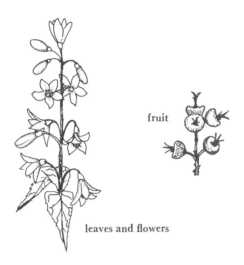

fruit

leaves and flowers

Deutzia gracilis is a graceful, dense, compact shrub with slender, ascending branches. It usually grows 2 to 4 feet wide, but may grow to 6 feet in height. Growth rate is fast. Texture is medium-fine in leaf; medium in winter.

The dull green leaves are deciduous, opposite, simple, 1⅓ to 1⅔ inches long and ⅜ to ⅝ inch wide, long, narrow, and coarsely toothed. The leaves do not color effectively in the autumn.

The stems are yellowish-gray-brown in color. The twigs are somewhat shreddy.

The abundant, scentless, perfect, single, pure white flowers appear in late May. They are ¼ to ⅓ inch wide, and are borne in upright racemes 2 to 4 inches long. If frost occurs before the buds open, the plant produces minute but otherwise apparently normal flowers.

The fruit is a dry capsule, and is not showy.

Deutzia gracilis is easy to grow, transplants readily, tolerates any good garden soil, and seems to be pH adaptable. It is preferable to transplant in the spring. The plant grows well in light to full shade, but the leaves will burn when grown in full sun.

To eliminate the tedious job of removing the old or dead stems individually, prune every 3 to 4 years to 1 to 2 inches above the ground. The plant should be pruned immediately after flowering; it will recover quickly from the severe pruning. *Deutzia gracilis* is quite hardy, but late frosts in low-lying districts may cause injury. Although this shrub is generally free of problems, it may suffer from leaf spots, aphids, leaf miners, and dieback.

Deutzia gracilis is widely grown. It may be used in the foundation planting, a mass planting, a permanent landscape container, in front of a shrub border, in edging a walk for traffic control, or in an informal hedge (plants spaced 2 feet apart). *Deutzia gracilis* is the first *Deutzia* to flower, and is perhaps the best selection of the genus. It is a more prolific flowerer than *Deutzia* × *lemoinei*. Although *Deutzia gracilis* is usually dependable for a delightful flower display in late spring, it is not especially outstanding the rest of the year. The summer foliage is a dull green, and autumn foliage color, fruits, and winter characteristics are not interesting.

Deutzia gracilis is easily rooted from softwood cuttings collected in late spring or early summer.

Its native habitat is Japan. The plant was introduced in 1840.

For a color illustration of *Deutzia gracilis,* see page 138.

leaves

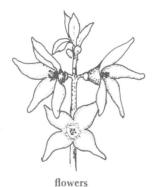

flowers

seed capsules

Forsythia viridissima 'Bronxensis' is a prostrate, compact shrub with masses of twiggy branchlets. The smallest of the forsythias, it may grow up to 2 feet high and 2 to 4 feet wide. Growth rate is slow. Texture is medium.

The dark-green leaves are deciduous, opposite, simple, oval, serrated, ¾ to 1¾ inches long, and are closely set on the stem. Fall color is green to yellow, and is not attractive.

The branches are often greenish and somewhat 4-angled.

The flowers appear before the leaves in April. They are small, primrose-yellow, 4-lobed, and singly borne. Usually the plants will not flower well, however, until after the second or third year. The flowers are abundantly borne on the inner stems of the plants, and are a welcome herald of spring. In cold areas, exposed flower buds may be killed during a severe winter. Branches can be collected in midwinter, brought into a warm room, and forced into flowering.

The fruits are woody capsules with winged seeds, and are not attractive.

Forsythia will grow in most soils, but needs full sun for maximum flowering. If the plant is multistemmed, it can be cut back rather severely; if it is single-stemmed, it should be "headed back." Since flowers form on the previous season's growth, the plant should be pruned immediately after flowering. It is not seriously affected by insects or disease.

Forsythia viridissima 'Bronxensis' may be used in the foundation planting, shrub border, group planting, as a ground cover on slopes, or as a hedge (plants spaced 12 to 18 inches apart). This *Forsythia* is excellently adapted to city conditions.

The plants can easily be propagated with softwood cuttings taken in late spring or early summer.

Forsythia viridissima 'Bronxensis' was raised in the Boyce Thompson Arboretum from *Forsythia viridissima* var. *koreana* seeds received in 1928 from the Botanic Garden of the Imperial University of Tokyo. Of the three plants raised, two were *Forsythia viridissima* var. *koreana,* and the other was a pygmy. Propagating material from the pygmy was given to the New York Botanic Gardens in the Bronx, and was named var. *bronxensis* in 1947 by T. H. Everett, the curator, who was unaware of the origin of the plant.

Hamamelidaceae (Witch hazel family)   Dwarf Fothergilla, Witch Alder

Zone 6

leaf   flowers   seed capsules

Fothergilla gardenii is a small, low, mounding, rather thin shrub with slender, zigzag, spreading branches. It grows 2 to 4 feet high and 3 to 4 feet wide, and may occasionally sucker from the roots. Growth rate is slow. Foliage texture is coarse, and the stem texture in winter is medium to fine.

The leaves are deciduous, alternate, simple, dark green on the upper sides and lighter green and hairy on the undersides, oval, 1 to 2½ inches long and ¾ to 1¾ inches wide. The petioles are ⅓ to ⅖ inch long and hairy. The somewhat leathery summer foliage is quite attractive. Autumn color is brilliant yellow to orange to scarlet, especially if grown in full sun. Often there is a combination of these colors in the same leaf.

The slender stems are rounded and zigzag. The young twigs are covered with white, starlike hair.

The white flowers are fragrant, cylindrical, 1 to 2 inches long and 1 inch in diameter, and are borne in upright terminal spikes resembling a large thimble. The flowers are apetalous (without petals); the showy parts are the stamens (white filament, yellow anthers). The unusual flowers appear before the leaves in late April to early May.

The fruit is a 2-seeded, dry capsule, and has no ornamental value.

Fothergilla gardenii requires a moist, acid, fertile, well-drained soil, and does not tolerate a heavy or poorly drained soil. Although the plant will grow in partial shade, it flowers and colors best if grown in full sun. It should be purchased as a balled-and-burlapped or container-grown plant. It is relatively pest-free.

This shrub may be used in the foundation planting, a group planting, perennial border, mass planting, in front of the shrub border, or in a permanent landscape container. It is especially attractive against a background of evergreens.

The seeds are difficult to germinate because they have a double dormancy requirement. The plant can be propagated from cuttings taken from suckers or softwood cuttings collected in late May.

The *Fothergilla gardenii* is closely related to the witch hazels. This genus was named after Dr. John Fothergill, who collected and grew many native American plants in his garden at Stratford-le-Box in Essex, England.

The plant's native habitat is from Virginia to Georgia. It was introduced in 1765.

For a color illustration of *Fothergilla gardenii*, see page 138.

Fabaceae (Legume family)   Common Woadwaxen, Dyer's Greenwood

Zone 5

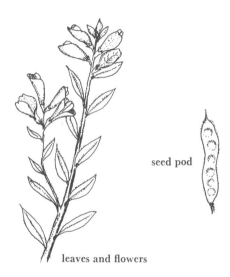

seed pod

leaves and flowers

Genista tinctoria is a low-growing shrub with slender, green, upright branches. It grows 3 feet high and 3 feet wide. Growth rate is medium to slow. Texture is medium-fine.

The leaves are deciduous, alternate, simple, up to 1 inch long, bright green in summer, and have no ornamental color in autumn.

The bright yellow, pealike flowers are ½ to ¾ inch long, and are borne on erect racemes 1 to 3 inches long. Flowering occurs on new wood, beginning with an abundant display of flowers in June. The plant continues to flower sporadically throughout the summer.

The fruits are pods that are not ornamental.

Genista tinctoria prefers a sandy or loamy, dry, infertile soil, and tolerates soils with varying pH. The plant is best grown in a hot, dry, sunny site. *Genista* is somewhat difficult to transplant. In the northern part of Zone 5, it may be necessary to prune the plant because of winter injury (twig dieback). Prune immediately after flowering. It is not seriously affected by insects or diseases.

This plant may be used in the foundation planting, shrub border, or rock garden.

Genista tinctoria is usually propagated by seed or softwood cuttings.

The plant received its common name, Dyer's Greenwood, in Europe because yarn dipped in a concoction of the crushed stems turns a brilliant green. The flowers are used to produce a yellow dye. It is the hardiest of the *Genista* species.

Genista tinctoria is native to Europe and western Asia, and has become "naturalized" in the eastern United States.

Saxifragaceae (Saxifrage family)

Annabelle Smooth Hydrangea

Zone 4

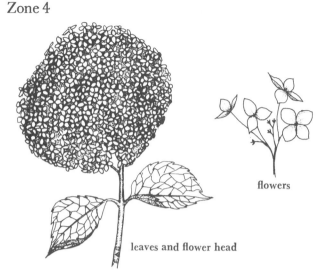

flowers

leaves and flower head

Hydrangea arborescens 'Annabelle' is an upright shrub that grows 3 to 4 feet high and 3 to 5 feet wide, and suckers freely from the rootstock. The many "shreddy" barked, arching canes branch after the first year. The young shoots are somewhat downy at first, becoming glabrous (smooth) as the plant matures. Growth rate is fast. Texture is coarse.

The large leaves are deciduous, opposite, simple, broadly oval or roundish, toothed, long-petioled, 3 to 7 inches long and 2 to 6 inches wide, and sharp-pointed, with a rounded or heart-shaped base. The upper sides of the leaves are bright dark green; the undersides are a paler green. Both sides are glabrous, or with down only on the veins or in the vein axils on the underside. The autumn coloration is green to brown, and is not attractive.

The numerous white flowers are crowded in flattened corymbs that measure up to 1 foot wide, and are borne from July through September. The nearly symmetrical flower heads are borne erect and terminally on the downy flower stem. The flower head is composed of many showy and nonshowy flowers. The nonshowy flowers have inconspicuous sepals, 4 or 5 petals, and 8 or 10 stamens. The showy flowers, usually arranged around the outside of the inflorescence, have a conspicuous calyx with 3 to 5 petallike sepals. The flowers open white, later turning green, and finally brown. They persist throughout the winter.

The fruit is a dried capsule, and is not ornamental.

Hydrangea arborescens 'Annabelle' grows well in partial shade in a rich, well-drained, moist soil. It does not tolerate dry soil, and does not grow well south of Zone 6. The plant is fibrous-rooted, and often requires supplemental watering during hot, dry summer weather. It is quite adaptable and transplants well. Because the flowers are produced on new wood, the plant should be pruned in the autumn or early spring. It is occasionally subject to infestations of the leaf-tying caterpillar that only attacks *Hydrangea*.

This plant may be used in a shady shrub border, near ponds or creeks, or massed in a shaded "naturalized" area. The flowers become so heavy that they can pull down the branches, creating an unkempt appearing plant when grown in the formal garden.

It may be propagated by cuttings of summer or dormant wood.

Hydrangea arborescens 'Annabelle' was named by Professor Joseph C. McDaniel of the University of Illinois. It has larger flowers than *Hydrangea arborescens* 'Grandiflora' (Hills-of-Snow).

Hypericaceae (St.-John's-wort family)

Zone 6

Sunburst Golden St.-John's-wort

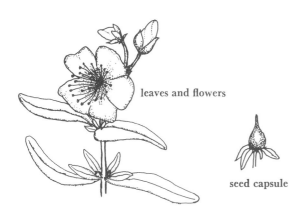

leaves and flowers

seed capsule

Hypericum frondosum 'Sunburst' is an upright, dense, low-growing shrub about 2 feet high and 4 feet wide. Growth rate is medium. Texture is medium to fine.

The blue-green leaf is deciduous, 2 inches long and ½ inch wide, simple, entire, opposite, and oblong, with numerous transparent glands. The autumn color is not attractive.

The plant has a weeping appearance because it often rises from a single stem of heavy foliage. The older branches are covered with a peeling, grayish-brown bark.

The orange-yellow flowers are round, 1½ inches in diameter, and 5-petaled, with a cluster of predominant yellow stamens in the center. The flowers are abundantly borne in clusters at the ends of the shoots in July.

The fruit is a 3-celled, broad-based, cone-shaped, ½-inch-high capsule with 5 large, leaflike sepals at the base.

During severe winters, the tips of the branches may die back, but damage is not severe because the plant flowers on new wood.

This *Hypericum* is one of the hardiest of the genus, and can be grown successfully farther north than any of the other species.

For a color illustration of *Hypericum frondosum* 'Sunburst', see page 139.

For a general discussion of *Hypericum*, see page 34.

Hypericaceae (St.-John's-wort family)

Zone 5

Kalm's St.-John's-wort

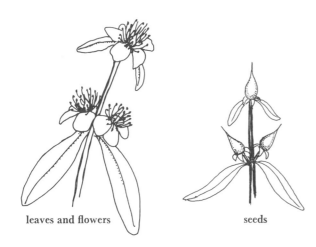

leaves and flowers   seeds

Hypericum kalmianum is a dense, compact, and rather straggly bush with many branches. It does not have the neat growth habit of some of the other species. It grows to 2 to 4 feet high and 4 feet wide. Growth rate is medium. Texture is medium.

The branches are 4-angled and slender.

The leaves are deciduous, opposite, entire, simple, 1½ inches long and ½ inch wide, bluish-green with grayish undersides dotted with transparent glands, and narrowly oblong. There is no outstanding autumn color.

The main stems are often gnarled, with dark-brown, flaky bark.

The bright yellow flowers are rounded, single, 5-petaled, and 1⅛ inches in diameter, with the characteristically predominant yellow stamens in the center. They are produced in 3-flowered cymes at the ends of the branches and in the axils of the upper leaves in early July.

The fruit is an oval, 5-celled (rarely 4-celled), dry capsule, and is not showy.

Hypericum kalmianum was named after Peter Kalm, the famous Swedish naturalist and traveler, who discovered the plant in 1750.

The native habitat of *Hypericum kalmianum* is the cliffs or rivers and lakes of Quebec and Ontario to Michigan and Illinois.

General Discussion of *Hypericum*

Hypericums grow well in hot, dry places and poor, sandy soils, with full sun and abundant moisture. After flowering heavily, the faded flower heads can be unsightly, and should be removed. Since this plant flowers on new wood, it should be pruned in early spring. Hypericums are short-lived plants. They are not seriously affected by insects or diseases.

Hypericums can be used in the shrub border. They have little ornamental value except when in flower. Their chief value is that they flower at a time when there are few other shrubs in flower.

Propagation is by soft-wood cuttings in late spring or early summer.

Oleaceae (Olive family)

Zone 4

Lodense European Privet

May also be listed as *Ligustrum lodense, Ligustrum lodense nanum, Ligustrum densifolium nanum*

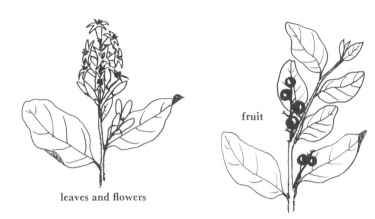

leaves and flowers

fruit

Ligustrum vulgare 'Lodense' is a low, dense, compact shrub about 4 to 5 feet high and 3 feet wide. Growth rate is medium. Texture is medium.

The glossy leaves are deciduous, opposite, simple, entire, narrowly oval, and 1 to 1½ inches long. They are semipersistent (remain green until December, then freeze and fall off).

The dull white, funnel-shaped flowers are ¼ inch long, and are borne in terminal panicles in mid-June. The flowers have a heavy, sweet odor that some people consider unpleasant.

The shiny black fruit is a small, egg-shaped drupe (stone fruit) that contains 1 to 4 seeds. The fruits are not eaten by birds, and persist throughout the fall and winter.

Ligustrum vulgare 'Lodense' is easily cultivated in any soil, and grows best in sun or partial shade. It is

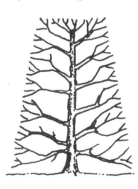

sometimes grown as a formal, clipped hedge. For best results, shear the plant into an **inverted keystone shape** (base wider than the top). Direct light is then able to penetrate to the ends of the lower branches, permitting the growth of new leaves after each shearing. *Do not* shear the plant so that the top is wider than the base or the sides are perpendicular. Because light cannot penetrate to the lower branches, the plant has little foliage at the base and becomes leggy. Do not try to maintain this shrub at an exact size. Allow it to grow 1 inch or more between each shearing so that it maintains a cover of new foliage.

When the plant becomes too large, it should be severely cut back to smaller than the desired size in February or March.

The plant is somewhat susceptible to twig blight (a fungus disease). Because there is no cure for twig blight, *Ligustrum vulgare* 'Lodense' should not be planted in large quantities in one area.

The plant is a compact form of *Ligustrum vulgare* (European or common privet). It is useful wherever a low, thick hedge is needed. Plants should be placed 2 feet apart.

Propagation is by softwood cuttings taken in late spring or early summer.

Ligustrum vulgare 'Lodense' was first grown in a nursery in the Rockford, Illinois, area.

Caprifoliaceae (Honeysuckle family)

Zone 5

Emerald Mound European Fly Honeysuckle

May also be listed as
Lonicera xylosteum 'Emerald Mound'

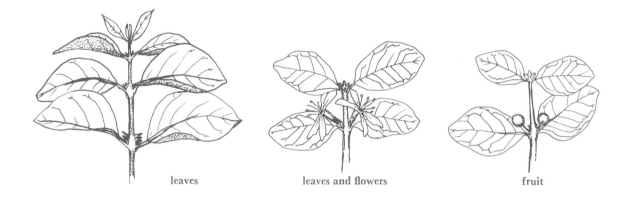

leaves   leaves and flowers   fruit

Lonicera xylosteum 'Compacta' is a low-growing, mounded plant about 3 feet high and 4½ to 6 feet wide. Growth rate is fast. Texture is medium.

The handsome, blue-green leaves are deciduous, opposite, simple, oval and 1 to 1½ inches long. There is no ornamental autumn color.

The funnel-shaped flowers are white with a yellowish tinge in the inner portion of the funnel, bilabiate (2-lipped or divided into an upper and lower part), and ½ inch long. They are sparsely borne in pairs in the axils of the leaves in early May, and are not fragrant.

The seldom-borne fruits are small, red berries, ¼ inch in diameter, that ripen in September and persist throughout October. Neither flowers nor fruits are showy because they are hidden under the foliage.

Lonicera xylosteum 'Compacta' is best grown in full sun, but will withstand partial shade. This plant will grow in almost any soil except wet soil. It will tolerate heavy pruning. Field-grown plants should be moved while dormant; container-grown plants can be moved at any time. The plant is not seriously affected by insects or diseases.

Lonicera xylosteum 'Compacta' tolerates city conditions, and may be used in the foundation planting, shrub border, or an informal hedge (plants spaced 1½ to 2 feet apart).

The plant roots easily from cuttings.

Bailey Nursery in St. Paul, Minnesota, collected propagating wood and named the plant *Lonicera xylosteum* 'Emerald Mound'.

Saxifragaceae (Saxifrage family)   Frosty Morn Mockorange

Zone 4

leaves and flowers   seed capsules

Philadelphus 'Frosty Morn' is hardy to temperatures as low as —30°F., and is able to withstand the coldest Minnesota winters without damage from freezing back. It is a dense, rounded plant 3 to 4 feet high and 3½ feet wide. Growth rate is medium. Texture is coarse.

The blue-green leaves are deciduous, opposite, simple, stalked, and entire. There is no autumn color.

The white flowers are very showy, double, and are borne on a terminal cluster. 'Frosty Morn' is one of the most fragrant *Philadelphus*. This cultivar is especially valued because the *Philadelphus* cultivars with double flowers make a greater floral display and tend to remain on the plant longer than those with single flowers. Flowering time is late May to early June.

The fruit is a 4-valved, dry, woody capsule, and is not showy.

Philadelphus 'Frosty Morn' was introduced by Guy D. Bush of Minneapolis, Minnesota, in the early 1950's.

For a general discussion of **Philadelphus,** see page 38.

Saxifragaceae (Saxifrage family)

Zone 5

Silver Showers Mockorange

May also be listed as
Philadelphus 'Silberregen'

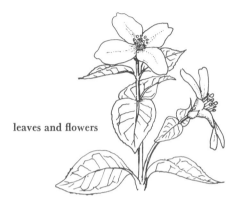

leaves and flowers

Philadelphus 'Silver Showers' is a dense, upright, narrow shrub that grows 2 to 3 feet high and 3 feet wide. Growth rate is medium. Texture is coarse.

The blue-green leaves are deciduous, opposite, simple, entire, stalked, slightly hairy, oval, and up to 1½ inches long. The leaves are not outstanding, and there is no ornamental autumn color.

The white flowers are single, round, very fragrant, 1¾ inches wide, flat, with 4 (sometimes 5) petals, and are borne mostly singly at the ends of the twigs.

The fruit is a 4-valved, dry, woody capsule, and is not showy.

Philadelphus 'Silver Showers' is a promising hybrid of recent German origin.

For a color illustration of *Philadelphus* 'Silver Showers', see page 139.

General Discussion of *Philadelphus*

Philadelphus require sun, and will grow on any well-drained soil. A plant growing vigorously in a good soil with adequate moisture and full sun usually produces the most and the largest flowers. Every 3 to 4 years, *Philadelphus* should be cut back 3 to 4 inches above the ground to remove the dead branches. Since the flowers appear from the previous year's wood, the plants should be pruned immediately after flowering. These plants are very susceptible to attacks from aphids and other sucking insects because of the sweet sap in the leaves.

Philadelphus can be used in the foundation planting, a shrub border, mass planting, and group planting. These plants have no attractive characteristics after the leaves have fallen. They are primarily of interest only during the two weeks that they are in flower.

The plants are easily propagated by softwood cuttings in late spring or early summer.

Philadelphus hybridize easily with one another in the wild and in cultivation. Many of the cultivars now available are the work of Victor Lemoine, a nurseryman of Nancy, France.

Rosaceae (Rose family)

Zone 2

Gold Drop Bush Cinquefoil,
Gold Drop Potentilla

flowers   leaf

   Potentilla fruticosa var. *farreri* is one of the
smallest shrubs of the genus. It is compact, dense,
and twiggy, reaching an ultimate height of 1½ to 2
feet, and spreading wider than it is tall. Growth rate is
slow. A 25-year-old plant at the Arnold Arboretum
measured 2 feet high and 3 feet wide. Texture is
fine when the plant is in leaf, and medium-fine
in the winter.
   The bright green leaves are deciduous, alternate,
entire, and pinnately compound. The individual
leaflets are less than ⅓ inch long, giving the plant a
refined appearance. Autumn color is green or yellowish
brown.
   The vivid yellow flowers are 5-petalled, ¾ inch in
diameter, and are borne in cymes from June to
October.
   The fruit is a plain brown, hairy achene that remains
on the plant until hidden by the new foliage the
following spring.
   Potentilla fruticosa var. *farreri* was introduced in
1920 by Reginald Farrer, who found the plant in
Tibet at an altitude of 8,000 feet.

For a general discussion of **Potentilla**, see page 42.

Rosaceae (Rose family)

Zone 2

Katherine Dykes Bush Cinquefoil,
Katherine Dykes Potentilla

flowers   leaf

Potentilla fruticosa 'Katherine Dykes' is an arching
or weeping, twiggy, irregularly mounded shrub that
grows 3 to 4 feet high and 3 to 4 feet wide. Growth
rate is fast. Texture is fine when in leaf, and medium-
fine in winter.

The medium-green leaves are deciduous, alternate,
pinnately compound, and entire. There is no autumn
coloring of the foliage.

The lemon-yellow flowers are 5-petalled, 1 inch or
wider in diameter, and are freely borne in small cymes
from June to October.

The fruit is a plain brown, hairy achene that remains
on the plant until hidden by new foliage the following
spring.

Potentilla fruticosa 'Katherine Dykes' occurred as
a seedling in the garden of W.R. Dykes, and was
named after his wife. It is possibly *Potentilla parvifolia*
(from northwestern China) crossed with *Potentilla* ×
friedrichsenii.

For a color illustration of *Potentilla fruticosa* 'Katherine
Dykes', see page 139.

For a general discussion of **Potentilla,** see page 42.

Rosaceae (Rose family)

Zone 2

Mount Everest Bush Cinquefoil,
Mount Everest Potentilla

flowers   leaf

Potentilla fruticosa 'Mount Everest' is a dense, twiggy, mounded shrub that grows 3 feet high and 3 feet wide. Growth rate is fast. Texture is fine when in leaf, and medium-fine in winter.

The dark-green leaves are deciduous, alternate, pinnately compound, and entire. There is no autumn coloring of the foliage.

The white flowers are 5-petalled, 1¼ inches in diameter, and are borne in cymes from June to October.

The fruit is a plain brown, hairy achene that remains on the plant until hidden by new foliage the following spring.

Potentilla fruticosa 'Mount Everest' originated in Holland before 1955.

For a general discussion of **Potentilla,** see page 42.

Rosaceae (Rose family)

Zone 2

Red Ace Bush Cinquefoil, Red Ace Potentilla

flowers

leaf

Potentilla fruticosa 'Red Ace' is a dense, twiggy, mounded shrub that grows 2 to 2½ feet high and 3 to 4 feet wide. Growth rate is fast. Texture is fine when in leaf, and medium-fine in winter.

The leaves are deciduous, alternate, entire, and pinnately compound.

The flowers are 5-petalled, ¾ inch in diameter, and are borne in cymes from June to October. The upper side of the flower has red lines running lengthwise through the petals, but the underside is pale yellow. The red color is usually disappointing, and fades out during dry periods or under intense heat.

The fruit is a plain brown, hairy achene that remains on the plant until hidden by new foliage the following spring.

This plant originated in England in the early 1970's.

General Discussion of *Potentilla*

Although potentillas tolerate light shade, they flower more profusely when grown in full sun. They will grow in dry soil, but perform best in a fertile, well-drained soil. Potentillas do not grow in wet soil. The plants tolerate heavy pruning, and should be cut back to 3 to 4 inches above the ground every 3 to 4 years to eliminate dead branches. Because the plants flower on new shoots, they should be pruned before the new growth starts in early spring. They are easy to transplant, and are not seriously affected by insects or diseases.

Potentilla can be used in foundation plantings, shrub borders, mass plantings, perennial beds, low hedges (plants spaced 1½ feet apart), permanent landscape containers, and as edging and specimen plants.

The potentillas are propagated by softwood cuttings collected in late spring or early summer.

The name *Potentilla* is derived from the Latin word *potens* (powerful). *Cinquefoil* is French for "five leaves," although some species of *Potentilla* have only 3 leaflets.

Rhododendron (Rhododendron family)

Zone 6

Coast Azalea

May also be listed as *Azalea atlantica*

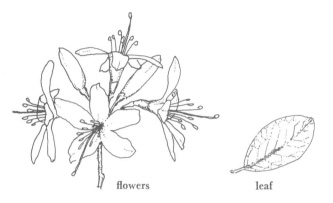

flowers   leaf

Rhododendron atlanticum usually grows 1½ feet high, but may reach a height of 3 feet after 30 years. The plant is twiggy, and spreads by horizontal underground stems similar to rhizomes that eventually turn into vegetative shoots aboveground. Growth rate is slow. Texture is medium-coarse.

The leaves are deciduous, oblong or inversely egg-shaped, light green or bluish green on the upper sides, and green or glandular and slightly glaucous (with a powdery or waxy bloom) on the undersides. The midrib is somewhat hairy, and the remainder of both surfaces is usually glabrous (smooth).

The flowers are 1⅛ to 1⅜ inches wide and 1⅛ to 1⅜ inches long, and appear in inflorescences of 4 to 10 in early May. They have a delicate, roselike scent. The pure white form is most attractive, but the flowers on some plants may be white flushed with pale violet-red (sometimes with a yellow blotch), light pink, or purplish pink. The hairy pedicles (stalks of individual flowers) grow up to 1 inch long.

Although *Rhododendron atlanticum* originated in a region of relatively hot summers with occasional dry spells, it grows well in damp woodlands. It is an excellent plant for open or shaded spots in the foreground of a shrub border, with low-growing, herbaceous plants, or "naturalized" under trees in a woodland setting. It is floriferous (flowers profusely) and very hardy, especially those plants collected from the northern limits of its native range. Since it flowers in the peak of the *Rhododendron* season, however, it will go unnoticed unless planted away from its more flamboyant rivals.

See pages 73-78 for cultural information.

The native habitat of *Rhododendron atlanticum* is along the Atlantic seaboard from southern Pennsyl-

vania southward to South Carolina, and restricted to the coastal plain. It appears most abundantly in Virginia and North Carolina, at low altitudes, and along margins of woods in which a single clone often appears in colonies as large as an acre.

In its best forms, *Rhododendron atlanticum* is a little gem among American azaleas. It was introduced to England in 1922.

According to certain authorities, the form of *Rhododendron atlanticum* described here is the plant growing in Virginia and the Carolinas. The original form of the species is said to be representative of the white-flowered forms found in Delaware. These are far more glandular than the typical *Rhododendron atlanticum*.

Rhododendron atlanticum is not included in the *Rhododendron* section of this book because it is a deciduous shrub under 4 feet high.

Anacardiaceae (Cashew family)   Gro-Low Fragrant Sumac

Zone 3

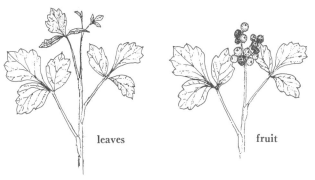

leaves   fruit

Rhus aromatica 'Gro-Low' spreads rapidly by rhizomes (underground stems), and by laying down branches that root at the nodes to produce a dense, tangled, irregular mass of stems and leaves. It grows 2 to 3 feet high and spreads to 12 feet wide. The plant may exceed these dimensions where the growing season is longer and warmer (Zones 6 and 7). Growth rate is slow to medium. Texture is medium.

The upright stems are slender, pubescent (hairy) and aromatically fragrant when bruised.

The leaves are deciduous, alternate, trifoliate (three leaflets), and are fragrant when crushed. The handsome leaflets are 1 to 2½ inches long, medium green to almost blue-green, glossy on the upper surface, pubescent, and toothed along the leaf margin. The petiole (stem of the leaf) is ½ to 1¼ inches long, and the leaflets are sessile (without petioles). The side leaflets are broadly oval; the terminal leaflet is the largest, and is elongated, 3-lobed, and oval. Autumn coloration is yellow, scarlet, or crimson, and is more vivid when the plant is grown on sandy, well-drained soil.

Within a given species, some plants bear perfect flowers (flowers with both male and female parts) and staminate or male flowers; other plants bear both perfect and pistillate or female flowers. The flowers are borne in dense, roundish clusters in mid- to late March. The staminate (male) flowers are borne in approximately 1-inch catkins, are persistent, and are exposed through late summer, fall, and winter. The pistillate (female) flowers are borne in short panicles at the ends of branches. The flowers are produced at the ends of short stalks on the current year's wood before the leaves appear.

The fruits, if present, are bright red, hairy drupes ¼ inch in diameter. They appear in small, tight, upright clusters in August and September (but only from those flowers that are perfect or female), and remain on the plant throughout the winter.

Rhus aromatica 'Gro-Low' is a good plant for poor, dry soils. It thrives in full sun or up to ¾ shade. Since the plant has a fibrous root system, it is easily transplanted, and is quite adaptable to most conditions. It tolerates pruning to 6 inches above the ground in early spring, and will grow back quickly in 1 or 2 seasons. For best performance, prune every 3 to 4 years. The wood is weak and brittle. This plant is not seriously affected by insects or diseases.

Rhus aromatica 'Gro-Low' is valued for its handsome foliage, flowers, and autumn color. It can be used on slopes and in other "naturalized" areas as a ground cover because it spreads rapidly by rhizomes, the stems developing roots wherever they touch the soil. This plant should not be used in a small area except in a permanent landscape container or contained by concrete or structures to keep it from spreading beyond established boundaries.

Propagation is by softwood cuttings in July.

Rhus aromatica 'Gro-Low' is the same genus as poison ivy (*Rhus radicans*) and poison oak (*Rhus diversiloba*).

The plant originated at the Burr Oak Nursery (Ralph Synnestvedt and Associates, Inc., Glenview, Illinois).

Saxifragaceae (Saxifrage family)　　　　Dwarf Alpine Currant

Zone 3

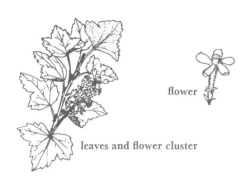

flower

leaves and flower cluster

Ribes alpinum 'Pumilum' is a densely twiggy, compact, spreading shrub that grows 3 feet high and 6 feet wide in full sun. The plant may exceed this height where the growing season is longer and warmer (Zones 6 and 7). Texture is medium-fine. Growth rate is medium.

The dark, shiny green leaves are deciduous, alternate, simple, 3-lobed (rarely 5-lobed), roundish or egg-shaped, and 1⅕ to 2½ inches wide. They appear very early in the season, and are retained throughout the summer in areas where the humidity is low. The yellow autumn coloration is not attractive.

The stiffly upright stems are shiny light brown to medium brown, with conspicuous ridges from the edges of the leaf scars.

Within a given species, some plants bear perfect flowers (flowers with both male and female parts) and staminate or male flowers; other plants bear both perfect flowers and pistillate or female flowers. *Ribes alpinum* 'Pumilum' bears both perfect and pistillate flowers. The greenish-yellow flowers are ⅛ inch in diameter, and are inconspicuously borne in racemes among the leaves in early April. The plant will flower abundantly during certain years and sparsely in other years.

The fruits are juicy, scarlet berries, ¼ to ⅓ inch in diameter, that ripen in June and July.

Ribes alpinum 'Pumilum' grows well in sun or shade and tolerates any good soil. It is easily transplanted, but is best handled as a balled-and-burlapped or container-grown plant. The plant tolerates pruning, and can be pruned at any time because the flowers are not an important ornamental feature. Leaf spot and mildew (brought about by high humidity and high night temperatures) and anthracnose (caused by cool, damp springs) can be serious problems in very wet seasons.

Ribes alpinum 'Pumilum' is an attractive foliage shrub that is especially adaptable for hedges (plants spaced 1½ to 2 feet apart). It can also be used in the shrub border or mass plantings.

Propagation is by softwood cuttings taken in late spring or early summer.

Ribes alpinum 'Green Mound' was introduced by the Burr Oak Nursery (Ralph Synnestvedt and Associates, Inc., Glenview, Illinois). It is reportedly a faster growing plant than *Ribes alpinum* 'Pumilum', maturing wider than tall.

Most plants in the genus (*Ribes*) serve as alternate hosts for the white pine blister rust, a destructive disease of 5-needled pines. The most effective means of controlling this disease is to eliminate the *Ribes* from the areas where 5-needled pines are grown. At least 15 species of pines are susceptible to the disease. Twenty-five states have been designated as "control areas" by the United States Department of Agriculture. Consult your county extension adviser to see if *Ribes* is quarantined from your area.

Rosaceae (Rose family)

Zone 5

Japanese White Spirea*

May also be listed as *Spiraea callosa* var. *alba,*
Spiraea japonica var. *alba*

leaves and flowers

Spiraea albiflora is a low, dense, compact, rounded plant that flowers profusely in the summer. It is a vigorously growing, multistemmed shrub with slender branches originating from the base. It grows about 1½ feet high and 3 feet wide. Growth rate is fast. Texture is medium. This species may not be as hardy as *Spiraea* × *bumalda* 'Anthony Waterer' (see page 47).

The leaves are deciduous, alternate, simple, short-petioled, lance-shaped, 2½ inches long, coarsely toothed, medium to dark bluish-green, and glabrous (smooth). The autumn coloration is not attractive.

The small, white flowers are profusely borne in rounded to flat corymbs (3 to 6 inches in diameter) in late June or early July.

The fruits are follicles (dried seed pods), and are not attractive.

Spiraea albiflora requires an acid soil. It will grow in sun or shade, but flowers more profusely in full sun. This plant has fibrous roots, and can be easily moved. Because it flowers on the current season's growth, it should be pruned in early spring before new growth starts. Removing the faded flowers will extend the flowering season. Every 3 to 4 years, prune the plant to 3 to 4 inches above the ground to remove the dead branches in the center. This plant is not seriously affected by insects or diseases.

Spiraea albiflora is valued for its white summer flowers. These appear when few other shrubs are in flower, and make a pleasing color contrast with the red-flowering *Spiraea* × *bumalda* and *Spiraea japonica* varieties. *Spiraea albiflora* can be used as "fillers" in the foundation planting, shrub border, a mass planting, or a hedge (plants spaced 2 feet apart).

Propagation is from softwood cuttings collected in late spring or early summer.

The native habitat of this species is Japan. The plant was introduced in 1868.

* The name of the genus is spelled *Spiraea* and the common name is spelled *spirea.*

Rosaceae (Rose family)   Anthony Waterer Spirea

Zone 5

leaves and flowers

Spiraea × *bumalda* 'Anthony Waterer' has an upright, broad, flat, compact habit, and grows 2 to 3 feet high and 3 to 4 feet wide. Growth rate is fast. Texture is medium-fine.

The young foliage is often pink-tinged when it first appears, later changing to an attractive green. The leaves are deciduous, alternate, simple, narrow, slightly toothed, 1½ inches long, and turn reddish in autumn.

The small, purplish red flowers appear in 4- to 6-inch flat clusters that appear intermittently for several weeks in June and July.

The fruits are follicles, and are not showy.

This plant is quite adaptable to landscape use because it tolerates both sun and shade.

Spiraea × *bumalda* 'Anthony Waterer' is perhaps the oldest *Spiraea* × *bumalda* cultivar. It was named after Anthony Waterer, the famous English nurseryman, and one of the first breeders of rhododendrons and azaleas.

For a color illustration of *Spiraea* × *bumalda* 'Anthony Waterer', see page 139.

For a general discussion of *Spiraea* × *bumalda* cultivars, see page 49.

Rosaceae (Rose family)   Crisped-leaved Spirea

Zone 5

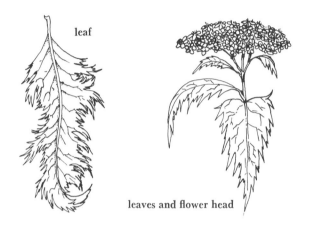

leaf

leaves and flower head

Spiraea × *bumalda* 'Crispa' is smaller than 'Anthony Waterer' (page 47), growing 2 to 2½ feet high, and can be substituted for the latter whenever a smaller, coarser textured plant is needed. It has the same growth habit as 'Anthony Waterer', but the growth rate is not as fast. Texture is medium to coarse.

The leaves are deciduous, alternate, simple, and twisted and greatly crinkled along the margins. The growing tip is red.

The small, bright crimson flowers are borne in flat clusters up to 4 to 6 inches in diameter in late June.

The fruits are follicles, and are not showy.

For a general discussion of *Spiraea* × *bumalda* cultivars, see page 49.

Rosaceae (Rose family)   Goldflame Spirea

Zone 5

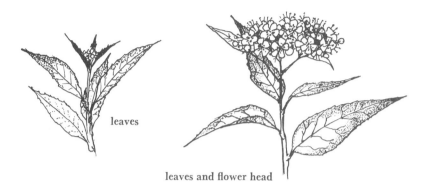

leaves

leaves and flower head

Spiraea × *bumalda* 'Goldflame' has an upright, broad, flat, compact habit, growing 2 feet high and 2 to 3 feet wide. Growth rate is fast. Texture is fine to medium.

The foliage is deciduous, alternate, simple, and slightly toothed. The spring foliage at the growing tip is red, turning to bright yellow as the leaf matures. The summer foliage is bright green. The spectacular autumn foliage is orange and yellow with red tips.

The small, purplish-red flowers appear in 4- to 6-inch flat clusters that appear intermittently for several weeks in June and July.

The fruits are follicles, and are not showy.

Spiraea × *bumalda* 'Goldflame' may be propagated by softwood cuttings collected in late spring or early summer. It may also be propagated by replanting the rooted offshoots because the plant spreads by underground roots.

For a color illustration of *Spiraea* × *bumalda* 'Goldflame', see page 139.

General Discussion of *Spiraea* × *bumalda* cultivars _____

The *Spiraea* × *bumalda* cultivars require sun to promote maximum flowering, and will grow in almost any soil. The *Spiraea* have fibrous roots, and are easily transplanted. Removing the faded flowers will extend the flowering season. The plants need pruning whenever one or more of the branches grow ½ foot above the others. Every 3 to 4 years, prune the plants to 3 to 4 inches above the ground to remove the dead branches in the center. Because the plants flower on the current season's growth, they should be pruned in early spring before new growth starts or immediately after flowering. They are not seriously affected by insects or diseases.

The *Spiraea* × *bumalda* cultivars may be used in the foundation planting, shrub border, a mass planting, hedges (plants spaced 3 feet apart), and as specimen plants.

Rosaceae (Rose family)   Alpine Japanese Spirea

Zone 5

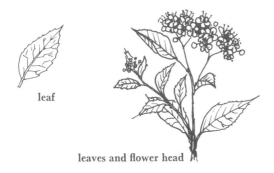

leaf

leaves and flower head

Spiraea japonica 'Alpina' is a tidy, dainty, low-growing, dense, mounded mass of foliage. Its ultimate size is 1½ feet high and 1 foot 8 inches wide. Growth rate is medium. Texture is fine.

The blue-green leaves are deciduous, alternate, simple, ¼ to ½ inch long, and toothed. The leaves remain green until the first hard freeze and then drop off.

The small, rose-pink flowers are borne in flat clusters that are 1½ to 2 inches in diameter. They flower for several weeks in early summer, and occasionally throughout the summer.

The fruit is a follicle, and is not showy.

Spiraea japonica 'Alpina' needs full sun, and tolerates any good garden soil. Mulching or mounding with soil is necessary to develop a multistemmed plant. The plant can then be pruned severely because the branches have rooted. If the single stem is severed, however, the plant is unable to rejuvenate itself. It is extremely susceptible to attack from aphids.

Spiraea japonica 'Alpina' may be used in the foundation planting, shrub border, a limited mass planting, group planting, or as an edging plant (plants spaced 12 inches apart).

The plant may be propagated by softwood cuttings in late spring.

Spiraea japonica 'Alpina' is one of the smallest of the spiraeas. It was introduced to America from England about 1958. Its native habitat is Japan.

unmulched plant

mulched plant

mulched plant with rooting of each upright stem

mulched plant with new growth after planting

Rosaceae (Rose family)   Crisped or Cutleaf Stephanandra

Zone 5

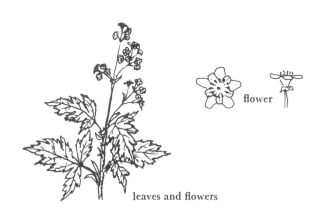

leaves and flowers

flower

Stephanandra incisa 'Crispa' is a spreading, dense, low-mounding shrub that grows 1½ to 3 feet high and 3 to 4 feet wide. Growth rate is fast. Texture is fine.

The gracefully arching branchlets root readily wherever they touch moist soil.

The leaves are deciduous, alternate, simple, deeply lobed, 1 to 2 inches long, finely cut, curly, and oval. They are tinted red when they unfold, later turning a yellow-green. Autumn coloration, usually red-orange or red-purple, is not spectacular.

The insignificant greenish white flowers are ⅛ inch in diameter, and are borne in loose terminal panicles in early June.

The fruit is a follicle, and is not showy.

The cinnamon-brown branches have an attractive zigzag pattern in the winter.

Stephanandra incisa 'Crispa' will only grow in an acid soil. It performs best in full sun, but will tolerate light shade. The plant requires an organic mulch for protection in severe winters. It is easy to transplant, and is not seriously affected by insects or diseases.

Stephanandra incisa 'Crispa' should be pruned in very early spring before new growth starts because the plant flowers on the current season's wood. It may show some dieback on the tips of branches during severe winters in the northern areas of its range.

Stephanandra incisa 'Crispa' is one of the best low-growing shrubs. It is usually grown for its dense, bright green foliage and graceful, arching habit rather than

for its flowers. This plant may be used to cover hillsides or banks, especially irregular rocky banks, because its readily rooting branchlets soon root and hold the soil, preventing erosion. It may also be used in the foundation planting, shrub border, on top of a wall, as a very low hedge (plants placed 1 foot apart), or as a ground cover.

Propagation is by root cuttings, seed, or division.

Stephanandra incisa 'Crispa' was found as a seedling in a Danish nursery in the late 1930's. It was introduced into the United States by Jacques le Gendre, Wachepreague, Virginia, in the late 1950's.

Ericaceae (Heath family)   Cowberry, Foxberry, Cranberry

Zone 5

leaves and flowers   fruit

Vaccinium vitis-idaea is a low, refined, compact bush with upright stems. It grows ½ to 1 foot high, and creeps by rhizomes to form broad patches of twigs and foliage over the ground. Growth rate is medium. Texture is fine.

The stems are densely covered with leathery leaves. The foliage is persistent as far north as Zone 6b, and is deciduous in Zone 6a. The leaves are alternate, simple, ⅓ to 1½ inches long, and egg-shaped. The upper sides are a glossy dark green; the undersides are paler and black dotted. Autumn color is metallic mahogany.

The waxy, white to pink flowers are campanulate (bell-shaped), 4-lobed, ¼ inch in diameter, and are borne in June on short, nodding racemes.

The fruits are bright scarlet berries with a persistent calyx, ½ inch in diameter, and ripen in August. Although they are acid and bitter-tasting, they make good jams and preserves.

Vaccinium vitis-idaea requires moist, acid soils and full sun. It usually performs better in a poor soil than in a fertile one. The plant should be cut back periodically to keep it dense and compact. It is not seriously affected by diseases or insects.

Vaccinium vitis-idaea makes an excellent ground cover in moist, acid soils. It may also be used in the foundation planting or shrub border with other broad-leaved evergreens.

Propagation is by softwood cuttings collected in late spring or early summer.

The native habitat of *Vaccinium vitis-idaea* is in moist, wet areas of Europe and nothern Asia. It was first cultivated in 1789.

Vaccinium vitis-idaea var. *minus* (Mountain Cranberry) is a native evergreen that forms dense mats 4 to 6 inches high as it creeps over the ground. Growth rate is very slow. Texture is fine.

The leaves are evergreen, alternate, simple, entire, leathery, and ½ to ¾ inch long.

The waxy, pink to red flowers are campanulate (bell-shaped), 4-lobed, ¼ inch in diameter, and are borne in late May on short, nodding racemes.

The fruits are dark-red berries.

Vaccinium vitis-idaea var. *minus* is very hardy. It can tolerate extremely cold weather in the north, but is unable to survive the hot, dry summers south of Zone 5b. The plant is difficult to establish in gardens, and the site must be carefully selected. It requires a moist, acid soil with adequate moisture and shade during the summer months.

Vaccinium vitis-idaea var. *minus* is better suited to landscape plantings than *Vaccinium vitis-idaea*. It is used primarily as a specimen plant or rock garden plant, but may serve as a ground cover (plants spaced 8 to 10 inches apart) in sites that meet the plant's cultural requirements.

Propagation is by softwood cuttings collected in late spring or early summer.

Vaccinium vitis-idaea var. *minus* is more commonly found in the United States than *Vaccinium vitis-idaea*. It is native from Labrador to Massachusetts to Alaska and British Columbia.

Caprifoliaceae (Honeysuckle family)   Compact Koreanspice Viburnum

Zone 6

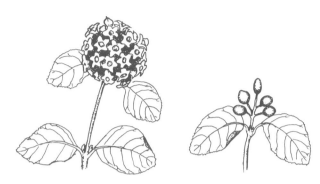

leaves and flower head   fruit

Viburnum carlesii 'Compactum' is a round, compact shrub, 4 feet high and 4 feet wide, with stiff, upright branches. Growth rate is slow. Texture is coarse.

The dark-green leaves are deciduous, opposite, simple, 2 to 3 inches long, oval, toothed, and pubescent (hairy) on both sides. There is no autumn color.

The tiny flowers are very fragrant, and are borne in terminal, rounded, dense cymes up to 3 inches wide. The flower buds are pink to red, but open white in late April or early May. This plant is more floriferous than the species.

The fruit is a blue-black drupe (stone fruit), ⅜ to ¾ inch in diameter, that is borne in clusters in August and September.

Viburnum carlesii 'Compactum' was discovered as a seedling in a Rhode Island nursery in the mid-1950's.

For a general discussion of **Viburnum**, see page 55.

Caprifoliaceae (Honeysuckle family)   Dwarf Fragrant Viburnum

Zone 6   May also be listed as
                                               Viburnum fragrans 'Nanum'

leaves   flower head

Viburnum farreri 'Nanum' is a dwarf, rounded shrub that grows 2 to 3 feet high and 4 feet wide. Growth rate is slow. Texture is medium to coarse.

The dark-green leaves are deciduous, opposite, simple, 1½ to 3 inches long and 1 to 2¾ inches wide, toothed, and slightly pubescent on the upper sides and in the veins on the undersides. The veins are prominently raised on the undersides and indented on the upper sides. The immature foliage, leaf veins, and petioles are reddish. The leaves are reddish in autumn.

Viburnum farreri 'Nanum' is usually the first *Viburnum* to flower. The flower buds, which are present all winter, are sometimes killed by unusually low winter temperatures. The small, white flowers are very fragrant, and are borne in terminal panicled cymes (1¼ to 2 inches wide) before the leaves appear in early April.

The fruits are attractive scarlet drupes (stone fruits), ⅜ to ¾ inch in diameter. They are borne in clusters in early summer, and are quickly eaten by the birds.

Viburnum farreri 'Nanum' originated in England in the mid-1930's.

For a general discussion of ***Viburnum***, see page 55.

Caprifoliaceae (Honeysuckle family)   Dwarf European Cranberrybush Viburnum

Zone 4

leaves   leaf petiole with disc glands

Viburnum opulus 'Nanum' is a dense, irregular, much-branched, tufted shrub that grows 2 feet high and 2 feet wide. Growth rate is medium. Texture is medium.

The fine stems are an attractive red during the winter.

The leaves are deciduous, opposite, simple, 3- to 5-lobed, 1½ to 2 inches wide and 2 inches long, maplelike, and occasionally pubescent (hairy) on the underside. The petioles have a narrow groove and large disc glands. There is no attractive autumn coloration of the foliage.

This shrub seldom flowers or fruits.

Viburnum opulus 'Nanum' may develop leaf spot (a fungal disease) in wet weather.

General Discussion of *Viburnum*

Viburnums tolerate almost any soil, except a wet, poorly drained soil. Although they prefer sun, many will flower and fruit in partial shade. Viburnums rarely need pruning, but will tolerate it. They are not seriously affected by insects or diseases.

These plants may be used in foundation plantings, shrub borders, low hedges, for edging, or as specimen plants. In hedges, space *Viburnum opulus* 'Nanum'

plants 1 foot apart, and *Viburnum carlesii* 'compactum' and *Viburnum farreri* 'Nanum' plants 2 feet apart. *Viburnum carlesii* 'Compactum' and *Viburnum farreri* 'Nanum' may also be used in permanent landscape containers.

The plants may be propagated from softwood cuttings in early June.

Ranunculaceae (Buttercup family)

Yellowroot

Zone 5

May also be listed as *Xanthorhiza apiifolia*

leaves and flowers

Xanthorhiza simplicissima grows to a uniform height of about 2 feet and spreads freely because it suckers from the roots. The erect stems fill the ground as a mat. Growth rate is medium. Texture is medium.

The roots and bark are yellow and bitter tasting. The Indians produced a yellow dye from the long, slender roots. The branchlets are pale greenish gray.

The handsome foliage is quite dense, especially at the ends of its upright stems. The yellow-green leaves are deciduous, alternate, pinnately compound, long-stalked, and clustered. The celery-shaped leaf is composed of 3 to 5 deeply toothed leaflets that turn yellow-bronze in the autumn.

The tiny, delicate flowers are nearly inconspicuous in late April or early May, and are borne before the leaves emerge. The flowers are ⅛ inch wide, star-shaped, brownish purple, and are borne in 2- to 4-inch, drooping racemes.

The fruit is an inconspicuous follicle.

Xanthorhiza simplicissima grows well in full sun or partial shade. It performs best in moist soils, but will grow in heavy soils. The plant thrives along streams and the moist banks of ponds. It may be transplanted in spring or fall. Old plants can be divided and spaced 1½ to 2 feet apart. The plant is not seriously affected by insects or diseases.

Xanthorhiza simplicissima is grown primarily for its foliage — the flowers and fruits are not showy. Because this plant makes a very solid, uniform, 2-foot mat, it is an excellent ground cover. It can be used under trees, to cover a moist, sunny bank, or to edge a shrub border. *Xanthorhiza simplicissima* should not be used in a small area unless physically restrained. The plant spreads rapidly, and could outgrow its allotted space.

Propagation is usually by division of old plants or by seed.

The native range for *Xanthorhiza simplicissima* is in damp woods and along streams from New York to Kentucky and south to Florida and Alabama. It was introduced in 1776.

Broad-Leaved
Evergreens

Ericaceae (Heath family)

Zone 2

Bearberry, Kinnikinick, Mealberry, Mountain Box

May also be listed as *Arbutus uva-ursi*

leaves and flowers   fruit

Arctostaphylos uva-ursi is a trailing, evergreen shrub with long, slender, leafy branches that form broad, thick mats. It grows ½ to 1 foot high, and may spread from 4 feet to 15 feet in diameter. Growth rate is slow. Texture is fine.

The young shoots are glabrous (smooth) or covered with a minute down. The exfoliating bark on the older branches is papery and reddish to ashy in color.

The leaves are evergreen, alternate, simple, entire, oval, ½ to ¾ inch long and ¼ to ½ inch wide, and are lustrous dark green on the upper sides and lighter green on the undersides. The leaf margins are hairy when young, becoming glabrous (smooth) with age. The petiole (leafstalk) is ¼ or less long. Autumn color is bronze to reddish.

The beautiful, white-tinged pink flowers are borne from late April to early May in short, nodding racemes. They are perfect, urceolate (urn-shaped), ½ inch or less long, and have a narrow, 5-toothed mouth.

The fruits are fleshy drupes (stone fruits) with 4 to 10 bony nutlets. The glabrous, shiny red fruits are ¼ to ⅓ inch in diameter, and are attractive to birds. The fruits ripen unevenly, beginning in late July and persisting through August.

Arctostaphylos uva-ursi is difficult to transplant. It should be moved as a container-grown plant, or by lifting the dense mats of branches in squares and transplanting them to a new location.

The plant grows best in a dry, well-drained, sandy or rocky, infertile soil with a pH in the 4.5 to 5.5 range. When the soil pH is above 6.0, it is necessary to lower the pH. *Arctostaphylos uva-ursi* is tolerant to salt, and is often seen growing wild on the beaches of Cape Cod. It is not usually seriously affected by insects or diseases, although black mildew, leafgalls, and rust have been known to occur.

Arctostaphylos uva-ursi shows a tendency to "fall away" from the crown. The stems often are not strong enough to hold the plant upright, and it sprawls, leaving an open space in the center that is not covered with foliage. For this reason, *Arctostaphylos uva-ursi* is undesirable as a ground cover for large, open beds in an important focal area of the lawn that is viewed at close range.

The plant is grown for its handsome foliage, flowers, and fall color, and is one of the best low evergreen ground covers for holding sandy soils (plants should be spaced 1½ to 2 feet apart). It may be placed on top of a wall or on steep slopes in naturalized areas, and is used along highways on the East Coast for planting sandy banks where little else will grow.

Arctostaphylos uva-ursi may be easily propagated by tip cuttings in late summer.

The native range is throughout the cooler temperate parts of the Northern Hemisphere in both the New and Old Worlds. It is found in diverse soils and habitats.

For a color illustration of *Arctostaphylos uva-ursi*, see page 140.

Buxaceae (Boxwood family)

Zone 5b

Compact Littleleaf Box, Kingsville Dwarf Boxwood

May also be listed as
Buxus microphylla nana compacta

leaves   leaves and flowers   female flower   male flower

Buxus microphylla 'Compacta' is a small, twiggy, dwarf boxwood that slowly forms a dense, compact bun. Maximum height rarely exceeds 1 foot. Growth rate is very slow. A 47-year-old plant in the Arnold Arboretum is 1 foot high and 4 feet wide. Texture is medium-fine.

The dark-green leaves are evergreen, opposite, simple, entire, thin, and leathery, and are densely borne.

The stems are slender, green, flat, squared, and grooved between each pair of leaves.

The pale-green, apetalous (without petals) flowers are small and inconspicuous. They are produced in early March in short, dense, axillary (in the leaf axils) or terminal clusters composed of a terminal pistillate (female) flower and several staminate (male) flowers. The staminate flower has 4 sepals and 4 stamens; the pistillate flower has 6 sepals and 3 pistils. The fragrant flowers attract bees.

The fruit is a 3-celled, dry capsule with shiny black seeds.

Buxus microphylla 'Compacta' may be used in the foundation planting, rock garden, or as a specimen plant.

This plant was discovered in 1912 by William Appleby of Baltimore, Maryland, and was introduced by Henry Hohman of the Kingsville Nursery, Kingsville, Maryland, in 1940.

For a general discussion of **Buxus**, see page 64.

Buxaceae (Boxwood family)   Wintergreen Korean Littleleaf Boxwood

Zone 5b

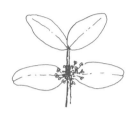

leaves   leaves and flowers   female flower   male flower

Buxus microphylla var. *koreana* 'Wintergreen' grows well in the Chicago area because of the moderating influence of Lake Michigan. It is a rounded, less dense *Buxus* that grows 4 feet wide. Growth rate is slow. Texture is medium-fine.

The bright green leaves are evergreen, opposite, simple, entire, leathery, large, and flattened. The green color is retained throughout the winter.

The stems are squared, slender, green, flat, and grooved between each pair of leaves.

The pale-green, apetalous (without petals) flowers are small and inconspicuous. They are produced in early March in short, dense, axillary (in the leaf axils) or terminal clusters composed of a terminal pistillate (female) flower and several staminate (male) flowers. The staminate flower has 4 sepals and 4 stamens; the pistillate flower has 6 sepals and 3 pistils. The fragrant flowers attract bees.

The fruit is a 3-celled capsule with shiny black seeds.

This plant can be used effectively in a "naturalized" site if it is allowed to go untrimmed.

Buxus microphylla var. *koreana* 'Wintergreen' originated from a collection or strain of 25 original plants. These plants were grown from seed obtained from Manchuria in the early 1930's by the Scarff Nursery in New Carlisle, Ohio. Unfortunately, because this plant was not propagated from a single original plant, there may be variations in growth habit and foliage color.

For a general discussion of **Buxus**, see page 64.

Buxaceae (Boxwood family)

Zone 6

Suffruticosa Common Box,
Suffruticosa Edging Box

May also be listed as *Buxus suffruticosa*

 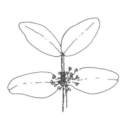

leaves   leaves and flowers   female flower   male flower

Buxus sempervirens 'Suffruticosa' is a dense, compact, slightly upright plant that grows 2 to 4 feet high and 2 to 4 feet wide. It is a true "edging" plant, and is the smallest and one of the most popular of the *Buxus sempervirens* varieties. Growth rate is extremely slow. There are 150-year-old plants in the United States that are not over 3 feet high. Texture is medium-fine.

The green stems are somewhat squarish.

The bright, shiny green leaves are evergreen, opposite, simple, entire, leathery, egg-shaped, and ¾ inch long. They are borne profusely, and are more fragrant than the leaves of other varieties.

The pale-green, apetalous (without petals) flowers are small and inconspicuous. They are produced in early March in short, dense, axillary (in the leaf axils) or terminal clusters composed of a terminal pistillate (female) flowers and several staminate (male) flowers. The staminate flower has 4 sepals and 4 stamens; the pistillate flower has 6 sepals and 3 pistils. The fragrant flowers attract bees.

The fruit is a 3-celled capsule with black, shiny seeds.

Because of its slow annual growth, this boxwood plant has difficulty recovering from severe winter injury (twig dieback). It is said to be least subject to attack from the boxwood leaf miner of any of the boxwoods.

Buxus sempervirens 'Suffruticosa' is commonly used as an edging to garden paths, flower beds, and shrub borders, especially those that are formal in design. This plant has been used in European gardens for centuries. It has been popular in the United States as a dwarf evergreen edging plant since colonial days.

For a general discussion of *Buxus*, see page 64.

Buxaceae (Boxwood family)

Zone 5b

Vardar Valley Common Boxwood

leaves   leaves and flowers   female flower   male flower

Buxus sempervirens 'Vardar Valley' is a dense, flat-topped, low, and compacted mound that grows to 2 to 3 feet high. It withstands temperatures to —20°F. It is one of the best low-growing forms for the Midwest. Growth rate is slow. Forty-year-old plants measured only 2 feet high and 7 feet wide. Texture is medium-fine.

The green stems are somewhat squarish.

The leaves are evergreen, opposite, simple, entire, and leathery. This plant maintains healthy green foliage all winter.

The pale-green, apetalous (no petals) flowers are small and inconspicuous. They are produced in early March in short, dense, axillary (in the leaf axils) or terminal clusters composed of a terminal pistillate (female) flower and several staminate (male) flowers. The staminate flower has 4 sepals and 4 stamens; the pistillate flower has 6 sepals and 3 pistils. The fragrant flowers attract bees.

The fruit is a 3-celled capsule with shiny black seeds.

This *Buxus* may be used in the foundation planting, rock garden, as a specimen plant, or as an edging.

Buxus sempervirens 'Varder Valley' was discovered in the Varder Valley of Yugoslavia in 1935, and has been grown in the United States since that time. It was introduced by the Arnold Arboretum, Jamaica Plains, Massachusetts, in 1957.

Buxus sempervirens 'Welleri' is another excellent cultivar similar to 'Varder Valley'.

For a general discussion of **Buxus**, see page 64.

General Discussion of *Buxus*

Buxus needs good drainage, and will grow in almost any well-drained soil. It may be grown in full sun or semishade. Plants in the northern area should be located where they will be protected from low temperatures, drying winter winds, and the hot sun in late winter and early spring.

Buxus should preferably be moved in early spring either as a container-grown or balled-and-burlapped plant. The plant is shallow rooted, and the loss of the feeder or surface roots reduces its ability to survive the transplant shock. For this reason, if you move a large plant from the location where it has grown for years, you should save as many roots as possible when the root ball is dug.

Pruning or thinning out some of the branches will help compensate for the loss of roots. The plant must be placed at the same depth at which it was growing in the nursery. Newly transplanted plants need protection from the summer sun to avoid burning.

The plant responds well to a peat or leaf mold mulch because the shallow roots require cool, moist conditions. Supplemental water is necessary in dry periods, and must be applied to the plants before they show drouth-stress symptoms. Do not cultivate over the root area — you may damage the shallow roots. *Buxus* may be pruned to maintain a formal hedge. If the plant needs rejuvenation, prune in the spring before new growth begins.

Most problems with the *Buxus* are man-made. It is of primary importance that the cultivar you select is hardy for your area. The shallow surface roots may be damaged by (1) cultivation; (2) improper planting depth; (3) excessive amounts of fertilizer; (4) mulch applied too thickly; (5) failure to provide adequate drainage when planted; (6) overwatering or insufficient moisture; (7) accumulation of dead leaves or ground cover at the base of the plant; and (8) soil eroding away from the plants, exposing the roots. The leaves and branches may be injured by toxic chemical sprays, shade, and the accumulation of gases or pollutants.

Buxus is poisonous, and should not be eaten by children or animals.

The *Buxus* are traditionally used in low hedges (plants spaced 1½ to 2 feet apart), along foundations, to edge formal gardens, in mass plantings, and for topiary forms (pruning the plants into artificial shapes).

Cuttings of the cultivars described in this book root freely.

The evergreen genus includes several European and Asiatic species. *Buxus sempervirens* is native to southern Europe, northern Africa, and western Asia. It was brought to the United States from Europe by the earliest settlers. *Buxus microphylla,* a hardier species than *Buxus sempervirens,* is from Japan, and was introduced in the United States about 1860. There are many varieties of both. The common name for this plant in England is "box"; the American Boxwood Society uses the term "boxwood."

The wood of the *Buxus* is hard, has a bony texture, and is used in wood engraving.

Aquifoliaceae (Holly family) Border Gem Japanese Holly

Zone 6

leaves leaves and flowers fruit

Illex crenata 'Border Gem' is a dense, low-growing, broadly rounded shrub that grows 3 feet high and 4 feet wide. Growth rate is slow. Texture is fine. It has survived winter temperatures of —8°F.

The dark-green leaves are evergreen, alternate, simple, petioled (leaf-stalked), lustrous, ⅝ inch long and ¼ inch wide, and dotted on the undersides with pellucid (minute, clear) glands. The tiny black specks on the undersides of the leaves are secretions from these glands.

The dull greenish-white flowers are borne in May and June, and are not showy. In most cases, *Ilex* are dioecious (staminate or male flowers and pistillate or female flowers are borne on separate plants). The staminate flowers are borne 3 to 7 in cymes; the pistillate flowers are borne solitary, and in the leaf axils of the current season's shoots. To determine the sex of a plant, it is necessary to examine it in flower.

The fruits are black drupes (stone fruits), ¼ inch in diameter, that ripen in September and October. They are rather inconspicuous because they are borne under the foliage. Only the female plants have fruits.

For a general discussion of **Ilex,** see page 69.

Aquifoliaceae (Holly family)   Heller's Japanese Holly

Zone 6

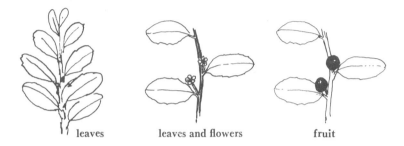

leaves   leaves and flowers   fruit

Ilex crenata 'Helleri' is perhaps the most attractive compact, small-leaved form. It is a low, dense, flattened, bun-shaped plant that usually grows about 2½ feet high. Growth rate is slow. A 26-year-old plant measured 4 feet high and 5 feet wide. Texture is medium.

The dull, dark-green leaves are evergreen, alternate, simple, petioled (leaf-stalked), ½ inch long, oblong, and have a few teeth on either side. The leaves are profusely borne, and are dotted beneath with pellucid (minute, clear) glands. The tiny black specks on the undersides of the leaves are secretions from these glands.

The dull greenish-white flowers are borne in May and June, and are not showy. In most cases, *Ilex* are dioecious (staminate or male flowers and pistillate or female flowers are borne on separate plants). The staminate flowers are borne 3 to 7 in cymes; the pistillate flowers are borne solitary, and in the leaf axils of the current season's shoots. To determine the sex of a plant, it is necessary to examine it in flower.

The fruits are black drupes (stone fruits), ¼ inch in diameter, that ripen in September and October.

They are rather inconspicuous because they are borne under the foliage. Only the female plants have fruits.

This plant may be used in the foundation planting, rock garden, a hedge, or a permanent landscape container.

Ilex crenata 'Helleri' is probably the oldest and most popular of the dwarf varieties. It originated in Newport, Rhode Island, in 1925.

For a general discussion of *Ilex*, see page 69.

Aquifoliaceae (Holly family)   Hetz's Japanese Holly

Zone 6

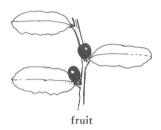

leaves   leaves and flowers   fruit

Ilex crenata 'Hetzii' is a dwarf, rounded shrub that grows 3 feet high and 4 feet wide. Growth rate is slow. Texture is medium.

The leaves are evergreen, alternate, petioled (leaf-stalked), 1¼ to 1½ inches long and ¾ inch wide, convex on top and concave below, and dotted beneath with pellucid (minute, clear) glands. The tiny black specks on the undersides of the leaves are secretions from these glands.

The dull greenish-white flowers are borne in May and June, and are not showy. In most cases, *Ilex* are dioecious (staminate or male flowers and pistillate or female flowers are borne on separate plants). The staminate flowers are borne 3 to 7 in a cyme; the pistillate flowers are borne solitary, and in the leaf axils of the current season's shoots. To determine the sex of a plant, it is necessary to examine it in flower.

The fruits are black drupes (stone fruits), ¼ inch in diameter, that ripen in September and October. They are rather inconspicuous because they are borne under the foliage. Only the female plants have fruits.

Ilex crenata 'Hetzii' is a clone of *Illex crenata* 'Convexa', and originated in the Fairview Evergreen Nurseries, Fairview, Pennsylvania. 'Convexa' is not described in this book because it exceeds 4 feet in height.

For a general discussion of **Ilex,** see page 69.

Aquifoliaceae (Holly family)   Compact Inkberry

Zone 5b

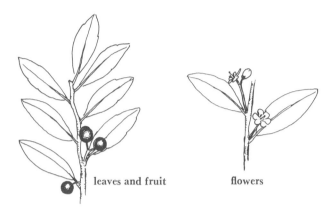

leaves and fruit   flowers

Ilex glabra 'Compacta' is a dwarf female clone with denser branches and foliage than *Ilex glabra*. It grows 3 to 4 feet high. Growth rate is slow. Texture is medium.

The glossy, dark-green leaves are evergreen, alternate, petioled (leaf-stalked), and 1 to 2 inches long. A hard freeze will kill the foliage and cause the plant to start dropping its leaves.

The female flowers are small, often dull white, with 4 to 6 petals, and are borne solitary in the leaf axils. They are not ornamental.

The fruits are black drupes (stone fruits), ¼ inch in diameter, and are profusely born when there are male plants of *Ilex glabra* in the area. The fruits ripen in September and persist until spring.

Ilex glabra 'Compacta' is an excellent plant for northern areas, and tolerates sandy shoreline conditions. It was discovered by the Princeton Nurseries, Princeton, New Jersey, in a group of seedlings.

For a general discussion of **Ilex**, see page 69.

General Discussion of *Ilex*

Ilex is a large genus of evergreen and deciduous plants that are usually dioecious (pistillate or female and staminate or male flowers are borne on separate plants). The flowers of all species are small and inconspicuous.

Because *Ilex* is dioecious, both the pistillate and staminate flowers must be present to ensure the pollination and fertilization of the pistillate flowers. Unfortunately, many nurserymen do not list the female and male separately. Make sure that you have at least one male plant to provide pollination for the female plants. To determine the sex of a plant, it is necessary to examine the flowers.

Ilex are not native in most areas of the Midwest. In areas where *Ilex* are native, windblown or insect-carried pollen may be sufficient to achieve pollination, and only the pistillate form of the species needs to be planted. It is usually safer to ensure fruiting by including both sexes in the garden. A small staminate plant can be planted in the same hole as a pistillate plant; then, as the plants grow, the staminate plant can be kept pruned to a small size and a minimum number of branches. Pollen from one species of *Ilex* may fertilize the flower of another species, but it is essential for the two species to be\in flower at the same time and in the same vicinity. The staminate plants must be within 40 feet to pollinate the flowers of the pistillate plant.

Only the pistillate plants bear fruit. In a favorable season, the fruits are borne abundantly.

Ilex grow best in a light, moist, well-drained, slightly acid soil. If grown in a dry, sandy soil, the plants should be mulched with oak leaves, pine needles, or composted organic matter. They adapt to sun or shade. *Ilex* are best moved in the spring. When transplanted in the fall, the leaves drop and usually grow again in the spring. Evergreen *Ilex* should be purchased as balled-and-burlapped or container-grown plants. The plants may be pruned after new growth hardens off. *Ilex* should not be sheared. In pruning, be careful not to cut the leaves in half; the portion remaining on the shrub will turn black. The *Ilex* described in this book are comparatively free of insects and diseases.

Ilex are attractive additions to the landscape because of their dense, stiff, twiggy branching habit. They provide interesting textural contrast to other plants in the winter. These plants may be used in foundation plantings, mass plantings, as hedges, and as specimen plants.

The *Ilex* described in this book are "root tender" when placed in an open site without the protection of a layer of mulch or snow cover. During the winter, part or all of the roots die, and the plants slowly die or are killed outright. For this reason, these plants should not be grown in a permanent landscape container or placed behind a retaining wall.

Propagation is usually by softwood cuttings.

Berberidaceae (Barberry family)

Zone 6

Compact Oregon Grapeholly,
Compact Oregon Hollygrape

leaves

Mahonia aquifolium 'Compactum' is a compact dwarf that spreads stoloniferously (a slender stem trails along the ground and roots at the node), and will form large colonies under proper conditions. It grows 2 to 3 feet high and 4 feet wide. Growth rate is slow. Texture is medium in summer and medium-coarse in winter.

The little-branched stems have gray-brown, glabrous (smooth) bark.

The evergreen leaves are alternate, odd-pinnate compound (5 to 9 leaflets, each 1 to 3 inches long), stiff, and leathery. They are lustrous dark green on the upper sides, and have slender, spiny teeth at the apexes and on the margins. The plant does not lose its leaves during the winter to as great an extent as the species, *Mahonia aquifolium*. Autumn color is a deep purple, changing to bronze.

The small, bright yellow flowers are conspicuously borne in late April on upright, terminal racemes 2 to 3 inches long.

The blue-black fruits are true berries, becoming decorative in August and September, and persisting throughout the winter. They are ⅓ inch in diameter, and are not poisonous.

Although *Mahonia aquifolium* 'Compactum' tolerates almost any soil except hot, dry ones, it grows best in a moist, well-drained, acid soil and partial shade. In northern areas, the leaves develop brown spots when exposed to winter sun. The old leaves drop in early spring, and new, unmarked leaves appear shortly afterward. This condition can be avoided by placing the plant in a site sheltered from winter sun and wind. It should be transplanted balled-and-burlapped or container-grown.

Mahonia aquifolium 'Compactum' can be pruned. North of Zone 5a, the plant responds more like a perennial than a woody shrub. The stems freeze back to the ground each winter, and must be pruned in early spring before the new growth starts. The plant is subject to leaf spot, leaf scorch, and attack from the barberry aphid and white fly.

It can be used in the foundation planting, shrub border, in front of taller broad-leaved or narrow-leaved evergreens, or as a specimen plant. The stoloniferous roots aid in holding the soil on a bank.

This plant is sometimes known as "hollygrape" because its compound evergreen leaflets resemble holly and its bluish-black clusters of fruit are similar to grapes.

The species *Mahonia aquifolium* is the state flower of Washington. *Mahonia aquifolium* 'Compactum' was introduced in Mount Vernon, Washington, before 1961.

Another cultivar, *Mahonia aquifolium* 'Mayhan Strain', is a selection from the Mayhan Nurseries, Veradale, Washington, and resulted from more than 25 years of selecting and growing plants from seed. Ninety-five percent of the seedlings do not grow over 1½ feet high. This cultivar can be maintained by seed propagation.

For a color illustration of *Mahonia aquifolium* 'Compactum', see page 140.

Berberidaceae (Barberry family)

Zone 6

Creeping Mahonia, Creeping Hollygrape,
Ash Barberry

leaves and fruit

flowers

Mahonia repens is a stiff, dwarf, suckering shrub that grows 10 inches high. The plant spreads stoloniferously (its slender stems trail along the ground and root at the nodes), and eventually forms small colonies.

The leaves are evergreen, alternate, odd-pinnate (3, 5, or 7 leaflets), dull bluish green on the upper sides, and gray and papillose (with small, nipplelike projections) on the undersides. The leaflets are oval, pointed, 1½ inches long, and spine-toothed.

The small, deep yellow flowers are borne in April in small racemes 1½ to 3 inches long, and are somewhat fragrant.

The black fruits are covered with a bluish bloom (powdery coating), ¼ inch in diameter, and are borne in grapelike clusters. They are berries, and ripen in August and September.

Mahonia repens grows best in a moist, well-drained, acid soil with full or partial shade. This plant shows a tendency to "fall away" from the crown. The stems are often not strong enough to hold the plant upright, and it sprawls, leaving an open space in the center that is not covered with foliage. For this reason, *Mahonia repens* is undesirable as a ground cover for large, open beds in an important focal area of the lawn that is viewed at close range.

Mahonia repens may be used in the rock garden, as a "filler" in the shrub border, or as a ground cover (plants spaced 1½ to 2 feet apart) in a woodland setting or other "naturalized" area.

The plants may be easily propagated by lifting and transplanting the creeping shoots.

The native habitat of this *Mahonia* is from British Columbia to Northern Mexico and California. It was originally discovered during the first Lewis and Clark expedition.

Mahonia aquifolium appears to have hybridized in gardens with *Mahonia repens*, giving rise to seedling plants with leaflets that are dull green on the upper sides and wider than either parent.

The generic name (*Mahonia*) commemorates Bernard M'Mahon, an American horticulturist who died in 1816.

Mahonia nervosa is a related species. It is a low evergreen shrub 1 to 1½ feet high, and is used as a ground cover or a specimen plant in the foundation planting or shrub border. Its lustrous evergreen leaves have 11 to 19 sessile leaflets in each leaf and large teeth on the leaf margins. The beautiful, bright yellow flowers are borne erect in 4- to 8-flowered racemes in late April. The purplish-blue berries (¼ inch in diameter) are showy in August and September. The native habitat of this plant is the West Coast from British Columbia to California.

Mahonia nervosa tends to winter burn badly north of Zone 6b unless it is sheltered from winter sun and winds. It is more readily available in the nursery trade than *Mahonia repens*, but *Mahonia repens* is more resistant to winter burn.

For a color illustration of *Mahonia repens*, see page 140.

Celastraceae (Staff-tree family)

Zone 5

Canby Paxistima, Mountain-Lover, Cliff-green, Rat Stripper

May also be listed as *Pachistima canbyi*

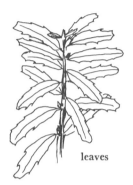

leaves   flowers

Paxistima canbyi is a neat appearing, dwarf evergreen ground cover with a dense, rounded mass of decumbent branches (reclining, with ascending tips) that often root when in contact with the soil. The plant grows 1 to 1½ feet high and spreads. It is one of the hardiest broad-leaved evergreens in the northern Midwest. Growth rate is medium. Texture is fine.

The spongy, slender stems are 4-sided and fibrous.

The lustrous, dark-green leaves are evergreen, opposite, simple, linearly oblong, ¼ to 1 inch long and ³⁄₁₆ inch wide, short-petioled, leathery, and glabrous (smooth). Autumn color is bronze.

The reddish flowers are inconspicuous, perfect, and ⅓ inch wide, with 4 petals and 4 stamens. They are borne in the leaf axils in early May in few-flowered, very slender-stalked, ½-inch-long cymes.

The fruit is a white, leathery, oblong capsule ½ inch long and ³⁄₁₆ inch wide. Neither the flowers nor fruits are ornamental.

Paxistima canbyi may be grown in full sun, semishade, or shade, but is more compact and dense in full sun. The plant requires an acid, well-drained soil, and tolerates long periods of drouth. This plant is easily transplanted, but is best moved as a container-grown plant. *Paxistima canbyi* rarely requires fertilization or pruning, and, once established, needs little attention. It is extremely susceptible to overwatering and to scale insect infestations.

Paxistima canbyi makes an unusual dwarf evergreen hedge or ground cover when spaced 12 to 14 inches apart. It may be used in the foundation planting, rock garden, to edge a path, or in a planter box or permanent landscape container. *Paxistima canbyi* is especially handsome in front of *Rhododendron*

plantings. It is not commonly grown in the Midwest, but is popular on the East Coast. Because the plant suffers from overwatering, it should not be placed in irrigated beds. Colonies may be allowed to "naturalize" in woodland gardens.

Propagation is by division in spring or by softwood cuttings in July.

Paxistima canbyi is native to the rocky, calcareous soils in the mountains of Virginia, West Virginia, southeastern Ohio, and northeastern Kentucky. It was introduced to the Royal Botanic Gardens, Kew, England, in 1893.

Rhododendron

Most hardy rhododendrons are native to the cool, moist regions of the Northern Hemisphere. There are no native species in the Midwest except in isolated areas. With the proper site, species or hybrid, soil preparation, and culture, you can grow rhododendrons and azaleas successfully in the Midwest.

The genus *Rhododendron* now includes the azaleas. The distinction between rhododendrons and azaleas is somewhat nebulous. The basic differences are as follows:

Rhododendron

Usually evergreen

10 or more stamens

Leaves are often scaly, or with small dots on their undersides

Flowers are mostly bell-shaped

Azalea

Deciduous, evergreen, or semievergreen

Mostly 5 stamens

Leaves are never dotted with scales, and are frequently pubescent (hairy)

Flowers are mostly funnel-shaped

Choosing the Correct Plant

The rhododendrons and azaleas described here can be grown in hardiness Zones 5b to 6b (see map on page 14). If you live near the northern boundary of Zone 5b, you must pay special attention to the culture and location of these shrubs in the landscape. They must receive the most protection possible from winter sun and wind. The microclimates in these areas may alter the hardiness zones for rhododendrons and azaleas.

Most evergreen azaleas are flower-bud hardy in Zone 6a, and flower profusely when quite small. The flower buds are set before the onset of winter. Damage results not from the winter cold but from early fall frosts that kill the flower buds before they are fully developed, especially when night temperatures in late August are not cool and the plant continues to grow.

Plants whose flowers are nipped each year by early frosts or that open some of their buds in autumn are not really adaptable to Zones 5b to 6b.

Do not buy plants labeled simply "rhododendron" or "azalea." These may have been propagated from plants with unknown genetic backgrounds, and probably will not be hardy for your area. Purchase only the plants described in this book unless you have thoroughly investigated the hardiness of other rhododendrons and azaleas and the adaptability of these plants to your home landscape. Consult the nearest chapter of the American Rhododendron Society, your county extension adviser, state land-grant university, or a nationally recognized arboretum.

Selecting the Site

Select a cool, moist site (preferably one that is partially shaded from 11 o'clock in the morning to 3 o'clock in the afternoon). Most rhododendrons are woodland plants. The shade of any tree except maple and elm is satisfactory, provided that the shade is not too dense. High shade under large oak trees that retain their browned leaves most of the winter or under large pine trees is ideal.

When rhododendrons and azaleas are placed under trees, the limbs should be pruned at least 15 feet above the ground. Thick canopies of large trees may be thinned to allow more light to come through. Do not overtrim. Once the limbs are removed, they cannot be restored.

Select a site on the north side of the house, garage, or other structure. The amount of shade needed is determined by the particular species or hybrid and the condition of the site. Plants with smaller leaves will adjust to higher light intensities; plants with large leaves require more shade. Protection from winter sun and winds is not as critical with the deciduous azaleas as with the evergreen rhododendrons.

The site should be well drained, lightly shaded year-round, protected from winter winds, and not crowded with trees and shrubs. Other plants compete with the rhododendrons and azaleas for space aboveground and water and nutrients belowground.

Mass the plants in beds — do not plant them individually in scattered locations ("shotgun" effect) around the landscape. Because deciduous azaleas do not have an attractive habit after the leaves have dropped and often become leggy, they should be placed in beds with other plants.

Preparing the Soil

Before planting, be sure that the soil is friable, well drained, and porous, and that it contains liberal amounts of humus. Incorporate a 3- to 6-inch layer of acidic, well-composted organic matter (by rototilling or hand spading) into the soil to a depth of 12 inches. Acceptable organic matter includes *acid* peat moss, decayed leaves, composted materials, and rotted manures. These materials may be used singly or in combination to comprise 25 to 50 percent of the soil.

The soil should be tested to determine the pH (see page 8). Rhododendrons and azaleas require an acid soil. If the soil is neutral to slightly alkaline (pH of 6.0 to 7.5), you can safely and slowly increase acidity by incorporating liberal amounts of composted organic matter. It is preferable to incorporate the organic matter in the autumn to increase the acidity before the rhododendrons or azaleas are planted the following spring.

If the soil is highly alkaline, excavate the area in which the rhododendrons and azaleas are to be planted to a depth of 10 to 12 inches. Set aside the topsoil and discard the underlying clayey subsoil. The clay eliminates air circulation and water drainage, allowing *Phytophthora* (a soilborne fungus causing root rot) to attack. Install drainage tile unless the bed is on a sloped site. Mix the topsoil with 50 percent or more acid peat moss. Replace the soil mix in the hole and allow the soil to settle before planting the bed.

Another method for amending the soil pH is to broadcast slow-acting flowers of sulfur over the bed and incorporate into the soil 1 to 2 years before planting rhododendrons or azaleas. Flowers of sulfur may be obtained from garden centers, florist supply houses, and drug stores.

The table on page 75 shows the correct amount of flowers of sulfur to be added for various pH's and types of soil. A soil test will indicate the pH and soil type in your area. Additional soil tests are not required unless the plants do not grow properly (discolored leaves, slow growth, etc.).

Iron sulphate (ferrous sulphate) is not recommended for acidification during the initial preparations of an alkaline soil because it can cause a buildup of

When a rhododendron plant is infected with *Phytophthora* (root rot), the leaves roll, droop downward, and clasp the stem.

soluble salts. When present in large amounts, these salts can be toxic to rhododendrons and azaleas. Supplemental water is alkaline, and may cause the soil pH to rise. In this situation, iron sulphate can be used in very small amounts as an annual topdressing to maintain soil acidity.

Aluminum sulphate should not be used to acidify the soils where rhododendrons and azaleas will be planted. Aluminum is toxic to these plants and will kill them. The leaves develop black spots, droop, roll, and turn brown. Terminal shoots and buds turn dark brown, then black, dying from the tip of the stem to the ground. These symptoms, which are similar to those caused by *Phytophthora,* occur uniformly over the plant.

If the soil is highly alkaline, iron (which is essential to plant growth and development, and must always be present in a soluble form) becomes a limiting element because it is insoluble at a high pH. The iron develops into an unavailable form in the soil, and the plant is unable to absorb it. As a result, the plant becomes chlorotic (the leaves turn yellow) and often dies. This disease, known as "iron chlorosis," may be corrected with applications of chelated iron as a foliar spray or soil additive. Chelated iron is neutral in reaction, and supplies the necessary iron to the plant regardless of the soil pH. This compound must be used according to the manufacturer's recommendations. Excessive applications will cause the foliage to burn.

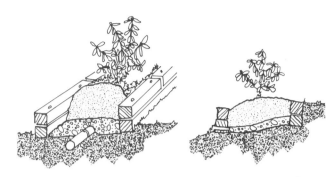

A raised rhododendron bed framed with railroad ties and drained with field tile (left). A simpler form of raised rhododendron bed using the natural slope for drainage (right).

Raised beds are often used to grow rhododendrons and azaleas. Lay out the area in which the rhododendrons are to be planted; construct retaining walls about 1½ feet high and 4 feet wide with rocks, bricks, or railroad ties; and fill in the bed with a properly prepared acidic soil. The soil mix for the raised bed should consist of equal parts of a good loamy soil, acid peat moss, and sharp, coarse sand. A raised bed prevents contamination of the carefully prepared acid soil by runoff (alkaline) water from the surrounding site.

If you have any questions about your soil type, preparation of the soil, or amendments to the soil, consult your county extension adviser or the agronomy or horticulture departments of your state land-grant university.

Original soil pH	Amount of flowers of sulfur needed to lower soil pH to 5.0 (ounces per 100 square feet)		Amount of flowers of sulfur needed to lower soil pH to 4.5 (ounces per 100 square feet)	
	dark-colored loams	light-colored loams	dark-colored loams	light-colored loams
6.4	74	52	112	75
6.2	66	44	104	69
6.0	59	39	97	65
5.8	53	35	91	61
5.6	46	31	85	56
5.4	34	22	72	48
5.2	21	14	59	39
5.0	—	—	38	25

Planting

Purchase only container-grown or balled-and-burlapped plants that are at least 2 years old. Larger plants become established more rapidly than smaller ones. It is best to transplant in the spring. Because of their shallow, fibrous root systems, rhododendrons and azaleas may be transplanted at any size in a favorable growing medium. The fine, silky roots do not tolerate poorly drained or hard soils.

Dig the hole deeper and wider than the size of the root ball, and place the plant at the precise depth at which it was growing in the nursery. If you place the plant too deeply, the roots do not become established because of insufficient oxygen, and the plant slowly dies. If you are in doubt about the proper depth, set the plant slightly higher than the depth at which it was growing in the nursery and mulch well.

When planting in an established rhododendron and azalea bed, discard ¼ to ½ of the soil removed from the hole and mix an equal amount of acid peat moss with the remaining soil before filling the hole around the plant.

Rhododendrons and azaleas should not be placed too close to a brick or stucco wall. The lime from the mortar leaches into the soil and raises the pH. Remove all buried construction waste, especially mortar and plaster.

Space the plants so that they will not be crowded when they reach their mature size.

A 3-inch mulch should be evenly distributed in the bed (see **Mulching** below).

Mulching

Suitable materials for mulch include hardwood bark, composted oak leaves or other organic matter, pine needles, and mushroom compost. Certain leaves, such as maple and sycamore, shed water, and should not be used as mulch unless they are shredded. Peat moss is not suitable as a mulch. It is difficult to wet; and once it dies, it blows away. The roots of rhododendrons and azaleas that have grown up through it become exposed to the air. Most uncomposted organic matter should not be used as a mulch because too much nitrogen is needed by the bacteria to decompose the organic matter, robbing the plant of its required nitrogen. If your plants show signs of nitrogen deficiency (yellowing leaves), add a fertilizer containing small amounts of nitrogen.

The depth at which a mulch is applied depends upon the material. For example, pine or evergreen needles should be applied 2 to 3 inches deep; whole leaves, 6 to 8 inches; shredded leaves, 2 to 3 inches; and hardwood bark or composted wood chips, 1 to 3 inches. The mulch must be replenished to maintain it at the proper depth.

Place the plant at the same depth at which it was growing in the nursery. Make sure that the bottom of the hole is firm so that the plant won't settle.

Form a water basin around the plant before applying mulch.

Watering

You may need to water during dry periods, even though the mulch and the organic material work to retain moisture. Do not wait until the plant begins to wilt. Apply water when the air temperature is rising. When the air temperature is falling (late afternoon or evening), the foliage remains damp, causing the plant to be more susceptible to disease.

Applying a fine mist to the foliage during periods of extreme heat will reduce the air temperature around the plant as the mist evaporates. The mist can be applied when the plant is in full sun without burning the foliage.

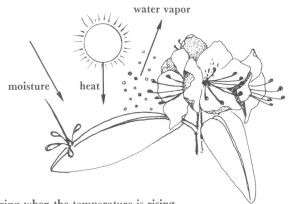

Watering when the temperature is rising creates water vapor that cools the plant.

Pruning

In general, rhododendrons and azaleas do not respond well to pruning. If you considered the ultimate height and width of the plant when you purchased it for a particular site, there is seldom reason to prune it. You may wish to prune your plants for the following reasons:

(1) to achieve heavier flowering the following spring by cutting off the flower heads before seeds develop;

(2) to remove dead wood or insect- or disease-damaged wood;

(3) to reduce the size of the plants and control shape by "heading back" larger, open plants.

When heading back, be sure that there are obvious growing points (buds) below the cut because the plant will not generate new buds on old wood. (See general discussion of pruning, page 11.)

After the flowers drop (top), snap off the seed capsules to allow the vegetative buds to grow and form new flower buds at the terminal (bottom).

Fertilizing

Applying fertilizer is not a substitute for proper cultural practices. Often the homeowner inadvertently kills rhododendrons and azaleas by overfertilizing the plants. An overly fertile soil produces lush plants that are less hardy. If you have only a few plants, you can use an especially mixed fertilizer for azaleas and rhododendrons. If you have a considerable number of plants, you may want to use a less expensive fertilizer that is low in nitrogen and high in phosphorus, such as 4-12-12 or 0-12-12, or a fertilizer that produces an acid reaction such as ammonium sulfate. The recommended rate is usually 8 to 10 pounds per 1,000 square feet or 1 ounce scattered in a 4-foot by 4-foot area around the base of the plant and lightly raked into the soil without disturbing the roots. The plants should not be fertilized after July first. Other fertilizers with different analyses should be applied at different rates.

Fertilizer must be applied in small amounts regularly because the plants are unable to absorb it in large amounts, and because it will leach from the soil rapidly. Apply in early spring before new growth starts, and again after flowering to ensure normal shoot growth and bud set for the following year.

In new plantings, it may be desirable to fertilize after new growth hardens but before July first. A high phosphorus and potash fertilizer may be applied much as a starter fertilizer is used on garden transplants. Older plants in a weakened condition (either pruned severely or damaged) may be given the same treatment.

Winter Protection

Rhododendrons and azaleas should be thoroughly watered in the autumn before they become dormant. The plants should not be allowed to dry excessively in the winter. Much winter injury results from dessication (drying out of the foliage). Dessication is caused by the inability of the roots to replenish the water lost by transpiration from the leaves during the plant's dormant period.

In cold areas, the soil under mulch does not freeze as early as an unmulched soil, and provides more constant and readily available moisture to the foliage later into the winter.

Antidesiccants may help prevent desiccation in sunny and windy sites, but they are costly, often difficult to apply, can burn the foliage if applied improperly, and may not last throughout the winter. One of the purposes of this book is to help the gardener grow plants so that artificial means of protection will not be necessary.

If you have selected hardy varieties and followed recommended cultural practices, winter protection from low temperatures probably will not be required. Evergreen rhodendrons need protection from the winter sun and winds. Natural shade, such as a pine windbreak or shade trees, should be provided. If the trees are not large enough to shade your rhododendrons and azaleas in winter, screen the plants with burlap.

Insects and Diseases

Except for weevils, the insects that attack rhododendrons and azaleas are easily controlled. The most common insect pests are the two-spotted mite, rhododendron white-fly, midge, rhododendron lace-wing fly, rhododendron clear wing, rhododendron stem borer, leaf roller, Japanese and Asiatic beetles, black vine weevils, strawberry weevils, and scale.

Disease pests may include bud blast, rhododendron blight, dieback, rhododendron wilt, root rot, and water mold root rot. Usually rhododendrons and azaleas are not affected by diseases unless the site is not suitable or the shrubs are old or incorrectly planted. It is more difficult to grow rhododendrons in the Midwest than in a moderate climate. With the proper site and care, however, rhododendrons will live for many years. Extremely low winter temperatures may weaken the plants, causing them to be susceptible to root rot, especially *Phytophthora*.

Positive identification of the pest and recommended control methods may be obtained by sending a sample of the infected plant material in a sealed bottle or plastic bag to your county extension adviser or to the entomology or plant pathology departments of your state land-grant university.

Propagation

Most rhododendrons and azaleas root easily from cuttings. These cuttings should be taken before the new growth hardens. Each rhododendron and azalea species and hybrid reacts differently to a particular method of propagation. NAA (naphthaleneacetic acid) and IBA (indolebutyric acid) are rooting hormones that are used in various concentrations ranging from 5,000 to 10,000 parts per million (ppm) to root these plants. Commercially prepared powders are excellent when a few cuttings are rooted. It may be necessary to experiment with various hormones in different concentrations and collect the cuttings at various stages of maturity for each species or hybrid. Most rhododendrons root well as softwood cuttings collected just before the wood hardens in early summer.

Ericaceae (Heath family)

Zone 5b

Boule de Neige Rhododendron

flowers

leaf

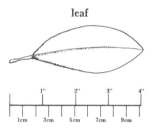

Rhododendron 'Boule de Neige' is a dense, compact, spreading, rounded plant that grows 3 to 5 feet high and 5 to 6 feet wide. Growth rate is slow. Texture is coarse.

The lustrous, dark-green foliage is evergreen. The leaves are 4 inches long and 2 inches wide, and are oblong to inversely egg-shaped.

The funnel-shaped, pure white flowers are borne in early May, and are a pale pink when in bud. The flowers are medium-sized (2½ inches across), but the trusses (compact flower clusters) resemble large snowballs. Each truss contains 4 to 10 flowers. The delicately frilled, compact, globular trusses nestled against the rosette of dark-green leaves are quite striking. The flower bud scales are persistent; the corolla is freckled with a few brown spots on the upper lobe.

Rhododendron 'Boule de Neige' is best grown in semishade because it is extremely susceptible to attack from the lacewing fly when grown in full sunlight. The most satisfactory method for controlling this pest is to move the plant to a semishaded site. When only small portions of the plant have been attacked, pick and burn the affected leaves.

This *Rhododendron* may be used in the foundation planting, in "naturalized" woodland areas, or as a dense hedge. It is one of the finest white flowering types.

Rhododendron 'Boule de Neige' is an Oudieu hybrid introduced in 1878. It is a cross between *Rhododendron caucasicum* and *Rhododendron catawbiense* hybrid.

For a color illustration of *Rhododendron* 'Boule de Neige', see page 140.

Ericaceae (Heath family)

Herbert's Azalea

Zone 5b

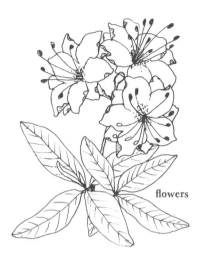

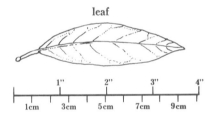

flowers

leaf

1"   2"   3"   4"

1cm   3cm   5cm   7cm   9cm

Rhododendron 'Herbert' is a low-growing, semi-evergreen, spreading shrub that grows 4 feet high and 4 feet wide. The flowers are dark crimson-purple hose-in-hose with a darker blotch, frilled, 1¾ inches wide, and are borne in early May. The origin of the plant is *Rhododendron yeodoense* var. *poukhanense* and *Rhododendron hexe*. The plant is very hardy.

Rhododendron 'Herbert' is a Gable hybrid. It was introduced by the late Joseph B. Gable, a well-known breeder of very hardy evergreen azalea hybrids.

Gable used a wide range of parents, but hardiness was established by *Rhododendron yeodoense* var. *poukhanense* (Korean Azalea) and *Rhododendron kaempferi* (Kaempfer Azalea). The selected hybrids are generally hardier than either parent. *Rhododendron* 'Purple Splendor' is similar to *Rhododendron* 'Herbert'.

For a color illustration of *Rhododendron* 'Herbert', see page 140.

Ericaceae (Heath family)

Zone 5b

Cloudland Rhododendron

May also be listed as *Rhododendron semanteum*

flowers

leaf

1"

1cm   3cm

For a color illustration of **Rhododendron impeditum**, see page 141.

Rhododendron impeditum is a low, dense, compact shrub with a rounded habit. Although it usually grows less than 1 foot high, it may reach 1½ feet in height under proper conditions.

The young shoots are an attractive blue-green.

The handsome, silver-gray leaves are about ½ inch long and ¼ inch wide, broadly oblong, and densely scaly on both surfaces. The scales are translucent at first, becoming golden with jagged edges when mature.

The funnel-shaped flowers are mauve to light purplish blue, ⅔ to 1 inch long, and are borne singly or in pairs from each terminal bud in late April and early May.

Rhododendron impeditum grows best in a cool, moist site. It may be used as a ground cover or as an edging for beds (plants spaced 15 inches apart), and in the foundation planting, shrub border, or rock garden. It is handsome in all seasons, and performs well under a canopy of larger trees.

George Forrest discovered this *Rhododendron* in 1910 in open pasturelands on the east and west flanks of the Leichiang Range, Yunnan, at altitudes of 15,000 to 16,000 feet. The plant was considered to be *Rhododendron fastigiatum,* and went into cultivation under that name. In 1916, however, it was described as a new species. *Rhododendron impeditum* is native to open, peaty pastures, forests, and cane-brakes in Szechwan and Yunnan, China. Its name means "tangled," and refers to its growing habit.

Ericaceae (Heath family)

Zone 5b

Karens Azalea

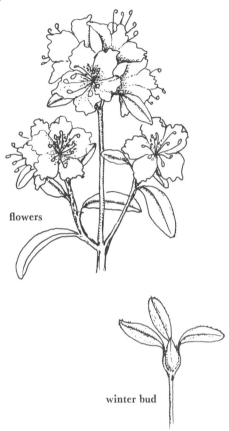

flowers

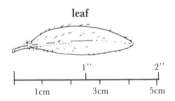

winter bud

leaf

1"   2"

1cm   3cm   5cm

**For a color illustration of *Rhododendron* 'Karens',
see page 141.**

Rhododendron 'Karens' forms a compact mound, spreading wider than high. It eventually attains a height of 3½ feet and a width of 4 to 5 feet. Growth rate is medium. Texture is medium.

The leaves are persistent; the rosette of leaves surrounding the flower bud remains on the plant during the winter. The lower leaves abscise (drop off) in January. The leaves are 1½ to 1¾ inches long, with pronounced brownish hairs on the veins of the undersides of the leaves and silvery white hairs on the upper sides. The petioles (leafstalks) are ¼ inch long.

The first-year wood is covered with brownish hairs.

The bright lavender flowers are tubular-shaped, 1½ inches wide and 1½ inches long, and are borne in late April or early May. They are clustered 1 to 5 flowers per truss, and will fade under extreme heat. The faded flowers remain on the plant after the flowering season is over.

Rhododendron 'Karens' flourishes well in many areas with severe winters. Because the flower buds mature in late summer, they are tolerant of the early frosts that are the most damaging to azalea flower buds. The wood is undamaged by frosts. The plant is tolerant of soils with a pH of 7.0. It is occasionally injured by the lacewing fly.

Rhododendron 'Karens' is one of the most adaptable rhododendrons for use in the landscape. It can be used in the foundation planting, shrub border, an informal hedge, a mass planting, or as a specimen plant, and it makes a fine floral display when grown beside *Rhododendron P.J.M.* (see page 84). Because *Rhododendron* 'Karens' flowers early, its color usually does not conflict with the colors of other rhododendrons, perennials, or shrubs.

Rhododendron 'Karens' is a hybrid azalea developed by Pederson Nursery, Wayne, New Jersey, about 1940. It is reportedly a cross between *Rhododendron hinoderigi* and *Rhododendron yeodoense* var. *poukhanense*.

Ericaceae (Heath family)

Zone 5b

flowers

leaf

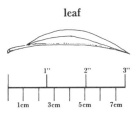

For a color illustration of **Rhododendron ✕ laetevirens,**
see page 141.

Wilson Rhododendron

May also be listed as *Rhododendron wilsoni*

Rhododendron ✕ *laetevirens* is a densely leafy,
compact, hardy dwarf shrub that grows 2 to 4 feet
high and 2 to 6 feet wide. Growth rate is medium.
Texture is medium.

The evergreen leaves are glossy, light green, and 2½
to 3½ inches high and ¾ to 1 inch wide.

The tubular-shaped flowers are pink to purplish, up
to 1¼ inches wide, and are borne in small clusters in
early June.

Rhododendron ✕ *laetevirens* tolerates sun but grows
well in partially shaded sites. It is extremely susceptible
to *Phytophthora* when grown in the Midwest, and
must be grown in a rich, well-drained, acid soil.

This plant may be used in the shrub border, rock
garden, or as an evergreen background.

Rhododendron ✕ *laetevirens* has longer leaves and
larger flowers than any other *Rhododendron
carolinianum* hybrid. The origin of this plant is
Rhododendron carolinianum ✕ *Rhododendron
ferrugineum.*

Rhododendron 'Pioneer'

Ericaceae (Heath family)

Zone 5b

flowers

leaf

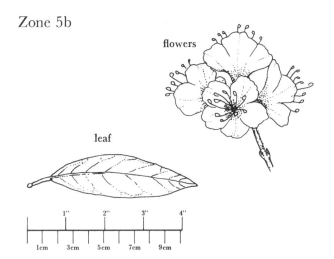

Pioneer Azalea

Rhododendron 'Pioneer' is a low-growing, upright,
multistemmed plant that may reach to 4 to 5 feet in
height after 10 years. It is hardy to −25°F. The
small leaves are semievergreen, and the plant is a true
Rhododendron. The light mauve flowers are borne
profusely in early April.

Rhododendron 'Pioneer' is one of the Gable hybrids.
The origin of this plant is *Rhododendron conemaugh*
✕ *Rhododendron mucronulatum.*

For a color illustration of **Rhododendron 'Pioneer',**
see page 141.

Ericaceae (Heath family)

Zone 5b

P.J.M. Rhododendron

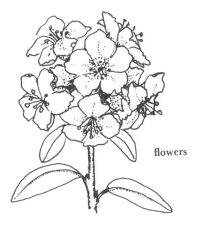

flowers

leaf

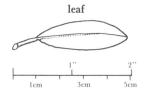

Rhododendron 'P.J.M.' has a broad, upright, bushy habit. It grows 3 to 6 feet high and 6 feet wide. Growth rate is medium. Texture is medium. This plant flowers reliably, and resists windburn even in areas where winter temperatures reach —20°F.

The thick, leathery, dark-green leaves are 1 to 2 inches long and nearly 1 inch wide, curly, and arch downward. They are glabrous (smooth) on the upper sides and rusty-scaly on the undersides. The leaves turn mahogany-bronze during the winter, and become green in April.

The bright, lavender-pink flowers are 1½ to 2 inches wide, and are borne in trusses (9 to 12 flowers per truss) in mid- to late April. The flowers are heavily borne every year when little else is in flower except forsythias, and cover the entire plant. The plant sets little or no seed.

Rhododendron 'P.J.M.' tolerates sun, heat, and cold. It thrives in sunny, exposed sites but can be grown in shade. An acid soil does not seem to be as important for this cultivar as for other rhododendrons.

Although *Rhododendron* 'P.J.M.' exceeds the height considered dwarf, it is included in this book because it is unquestionably one of the best rhododendrons for Midwest conditions.

Rhododendron 'P.J.M.' can be used in the foundation planting, shrub border, a woodland planting, or as a specimen plant.

This plant originated in 1943 in the Weston Nursery, Hopkinton, Massachusetts, and was named after the owner, Peter J. Mezzitt. The origin of this plant is *Rhododendron carolinianum* × *Rhododendron dauricum sempervirens*. Several strains with slightly different genetic makeups have been introduced under the name *Rhododendron* 'P.J.M.', resulting in minor variations in hardiness, growth habit, and flower form and color. Of particular importance is the fact that some strains are hardier than others.

For a color illustration of *Rhododendron* 'P.J.M.', see page 142.

Ericaceae (Heath family)

Zone 5b

Purple Gem Rhododendron

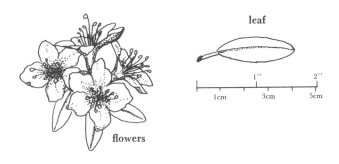

For a color illustration of *Rhododendron* 'Purple Gem', see page 142.

Rhododendron 'Purple Gem' is a low, compact, rounded dwarf that grows 2½ feet high and slightly less in diameter. Growth rate is slow. Texture is fine.

The leaves are evergreen, small, medium-green, and scalelike, and turn bronze in winter. The new foliage is a lovely bluish color.

The plant is covered with masses of light purple flowers in late April.

It tolerates full sun, and can be used in the foundation planting and shrub border.

Rhododendron 'Purple Gem' is a Guy G. Nearing hybrid. The origin of this plant is *Rhododendron fastigiatum* × *Rhododendron carolinianum*. It is similar to *Rhododendron* 'Ramapo'.

Rhododendron 'Ramapo'

Ericaceae (Heath family)

Zone 5b

Ramapo Rhododendron

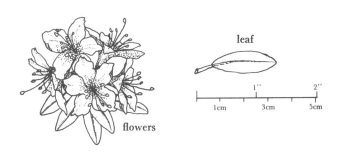

For a color illustration of *Rhododendron* 'Ramapo', see page 142.

Rhododendron 'Ramapo' is one of the truly hardy dwarf rhododendrons, growing only 2 feet high and 4 feet wide.

The small, evergreen leaves are a dusty blue on new growth, later turning an attractive blue-green.

This plant is often referred to as a "blue *Rhododendron*" because of its bright, light-violet flowers. The flowers are borne profusely in early April.

Rhododendron 'Ramapo' can be grown in sun or partial shade, but remains more compact in full sun.

It is well suited for use in the shrub border, rock garden, or as an edging plant, and is an outstanding specimen plant in all seasons.

Ericaceae (Heath family)

Zone 5b

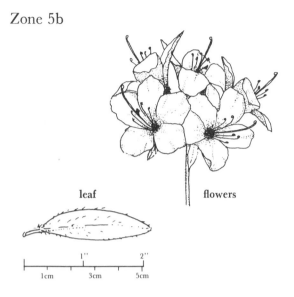

leaf   flowers

1"   2"
1cm   3cm   5cm

Stewart's Azalea

Rhododendron 'Stewartstonian' is a very hardy plant with a compact, bushy habit. Its small, dark-green foliage turns wine red in autumn. The flowers are bright, clear red. It grows 4 feet high and 4 feet wide.

This evergreen azalea is one of the Gable hybrids.

For a color illustration of *Rhododendron* 'Stewartstonian', see page 142.

Rhododendron 'Windbeam'

Ericaceae (Heath family)

Zone 5b

leaf   flowers

1"   2"
1cm   3cm   5cm

For a color illustration of *Rhododendron* 'Windbeam', see page 142.

Windbeam Rhododendron

Rhododendron 'Windbeam' is a semidwarf shrub that can become somewhat sprawly because of its long, willowy shoots. It is 4 feet high and 4 feet wide at maturity. This plant flowers after winters of −20°F. Growth rate is slow. Texture is medium.

The leaves are evergreen, round, small, highly aromatic, and do not curl until the temperature dips far below zero.

The flowers appear as light pink, changing to a deeper pink in early May. The plant sets flower buds at an early age.

Rhododendron 'Windbeam' tolerates full sun, and is easy to grow.

The beauty of this plant rivals that of the more tender, exotic rhododendrons. It can be used as a specimen plant in the foundation planting or shrub border.

Rhododendron 'Windbeam' is a Guy G. Nearing hybrid. It originated from open-pollinated seedlings of a Gable hybrid, *Rhododendron* 'Conestoga' (*Rhododendron carolinianum* × *Rhododendron racemosum*).

Ericaceae (Heath family)

Zone 5b

Yak Rhododendron

May also be listed as *Rhododendron* var. *yakusimanum*

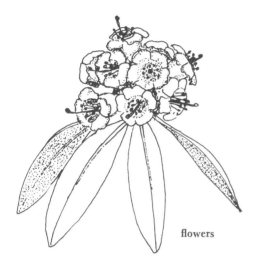

flowers

leaf

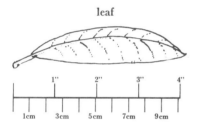

Rhododendron yakusimanum is a low, dense, spreading, rounded shrub that forms a perfect mound and grows 3 feet high and 3 feet wide. Growth rate is slow. Texture is coarse. It is hardy to —24°F. in open frames.

The handsome, glossy, gray-green leaves are evergreen, and have a heavy brownish indumentum (covering of hairs) on the undersides. The leaves are up to 3½ inches long and 1½ inches wide, and the edges are recurved. The upper sides of the leaves are often irregularly dusted with a mealy, whitish extension of indumentum that profusely covers the petioles and decorates the young shoots.

The campanulate (bell-shaped) flowers are 1¾ inches wide, and are freely borne in late May, usually with 5-lobed corolla. The buds are bright rose; the flowers may be rose, fresh pink, or white. The flowers of some plants open pink, fading to pure white; others open pure white or open and remain pale pink. About 10 flowers are clustered in a firm, dome-shaped truss.

Rhododendron yakusimanum requires a protected spot from the wind, but grows well in full sun.

This popular *Rhododendron* has a nearly perfect growth habit. It can be used in the foundation planting, for edging, as a ground cover, or as a specimen plant.

Rhododendron yakusimanum is only native to Yaku Shima Island in southern Japan, where it grows on or below the tops of the peaks from 4,000 to 6,000 feet. The climatological zones over the various altitudes have produced wide variations in the species. Some forms are found growing 25 feet high in forests; other low-growing or prostrate forms with strongly revolute leaves (rolled downward) grow in exposed places.

Rhododendron yakusimanum is subjected to heavy precipitation in its native habitat. It is one of the first plants to grow after a volcano has erupted.

This plant can be easily propagated by softwood cuttings.

Takenoshin Nakai discovered the plant in 1921. *Rhododendron yakusimanum* became known in England when Lionel de Rothschild received two plants at Exbury in the mid-1930's.

Some of the fine cultivars of *Rhododendron yakusimanum* include 'Ken Janek', 'Koichiro Wada', 'Mist Maiden', 'Whitney form', 'Yak-ity-yak', 'Yaku Angel', 'Yaku Duchess', 'Yaku Duke', 'Yaku King', 'Yaku Prince', 'Yaku Princess', and 'Yaku Queen.'

For color illustrations of *Rhododendron yakusimanum*, see page 143.

Ericaceae (Heath family)   Korean Azalea

Zone 5b

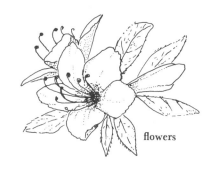

flowers

leaf

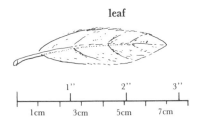

1"	2"	3"
1cm 3cm	5cm	7cm

Rhododendron yeodoense var. *poukhanense* is a compact, low-growing shrub that forms a broad, dense mat on exposed sites, but is more loosely branched in shady sites. This hardy species usually grows to about 3 feet high, rarely to 6 feet. Growth rate is medium. Texture is coarse.

The young shoots are covered with appressed (flat) bristles.

The leaves are persistent in the north, and evergreen in the south. The plant has dimorphic leaves (small winter leaves and large summer leaves), thus retaining a somewhat evergreen nature. The pointed leaves grow up to 3½ inches long (usually less), and 1 inch wide, and are dark green in summer. Both leaf surfaces are bristly, especially at the margin. Autumn coloration is orange and red.

This floriferous plant is covered in mid-May with rose to pale lilac-purple flowers that are freely spotted on the upper lobes. The fragrant flowers are single, broadly funnel-shaped, 1½ to 2½ inches wide, and are borne 2 or more per truss either before or as the leaves appear. The bristly pedicle (flowerstalk) is ⅓ inch long. The plant is free flowering even when quite small. Early fall frosts can kill the flower buds.

The common lilac-purple color can be striking in a garden if the plant is placed among green foliage and not in proximity to other plants with brightly colored flowers. This azalea flowers early enough to be free from clashing with other azaleas. The flowers are attractive when grown near white, light yellow, or green, but may appear dull in competition with brighter colors. The plant contrasts pleasingly with *Cornus florida* (Flowering Dogwood), which flowers about the same time. Joseph Gable improved the color of *Rhododendron yeodoense* var. *poukhanense* by crossing it with other brightly colored species of rhododendrons. It is frequently used as a parent in the Gable hybrids.

The native habitat of *Rhododendron yeodoense* var. *poukhanense* is around waterways and on hilltops in central and southern Korea, the islands off the Korean coasts, and the Tsushima Islands off Poukhan, Kyusky, Japan. Although the plant is named for Mount Korea, it is not common in that area. It was introduced to the Arnold Arboretum, Jamaica Plains, Massachusetts, by J. G. Jack in 1905. Introduction to England followed in 1913.

For color illustrations of *Rhododendron yeodoense* var. *poukhanense,* see page 143.

Needle
Evergreens
(Dwarf Conifers)

A **conifer** is a cone-bearing plant. A dwarf conifer never attains the height typical of the species from which it is derived. For example, a very old, 20-foot-high dwarf conifer could be derived from a plant with a height of more than 100 feet. Most of the dwarf conifers discussed in this book reach a height of 4 feet or less. Extremely small conifers (some plants may be only 12 inches high and 8 inches wide after 25 years of growth) are not included because they are unsuitable for landscape use.

The nomenclature (universal botanical names) of the dwarf conifers has been confused for many years. A plant may be found under its current name in one nursery and under an obsolete name in another. To help you locate the plants discussed here, we have included both the current and obsolete names for a plant whenever possible. These names are adapted from those listed in *Manual for Cultivated Cultivars* by den Ouden and Boom.

Physical Characteristics

The dwarf conifers vary considerably in growth habit. They may be pyramidal, vase-shaped, umbellate (umbrella-shaped), globose, prostrate, weeping, or irregular, contorted forms.

Conifers bear three types of leaves: awl-shaped or "juvenile"; scalelike or "mature"; and needlelike foliage.

The **awl-shaped leaves** are slender, delicate spines that taper to a needlelike point, and are usually quite sharp. These leaves are the first to develop on certain conifer seedlings, and are commonly called "juvenile" leaves. They may appear, however, on a plant of any age, on the same twig with scalelike or "mature" leaves, or they may be the only leaves that the plant bears throughout its lifetime. The awl-shaped leaves are especially prevalent among the juniper species.

The **scalelike or "mature" leaves** appear at the tips of the branches each spring. These leaves are closely appressed to the twig, and are usually soft to the touch. They commonly appear on *Juniperus* (juniper), *Chamaecyparis* (false cypress), and *Thuja* (arborvitae).

Needlelike foliage is the third leaf type found on conifers. The needles vary in size, and may be flat, circular, or angular in cross-section. *Abies* (fir), *Tsuga* (hemlock), and *Picea* (spruce) usually bear the needles singly or in clusters along the stem; *Pinus* (pine) usually bears the leaves in fascicles (clusters) of 2, 3, 2 and 3, or 5.

Growth Habits

columnar

pyramidal

globose

weeping

irregular

umbellate

prostrate

Dwarf Conifer Leaves

Scalelike Leaves

Needlelike Leaves

Juniperus chinensis
var. *sargentii*

Juniperus
conferta

Juniperus
procumbens

arborvitae

false cypress

pine
(2-needled bundle,
twisted)

hemlock

pine
(2-needled bundle)

pine
(3-needled bundle)

pine
(5-needled bundle)

fir needles
on a stem

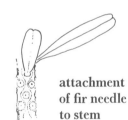

attachment
of fir needle
to stem

cross-section
of fir needle

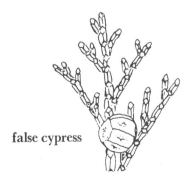

spruce needles
on a stem

attachment
of spruce needle
to stem

cross-section
of spruce needle

The flowers are always unisexual. The staminate or male flowers are borne in cones or catkins on the main axis, and the pistillate or female flowers are borne in cones with naked ovules (egg-containing units of the ovary that become the seed after fertilization).

The typical cone-bearing plants include pine, hemlock, fir, spruce, and arborvitae. The seeds develop on the scales that make up the cones. Certain conifers (including false cypress, juniper, and *Taxus* or yew) form seeds in small, more or less fleshy "fruits" that are modified cones. The fruits of most conifers ripen from September to November. The cones of pines usually require 2 years to reach maturity.

Cultural Practices

Dwarf conifers and other small plants should be planted in an open site, away from larger plants. Because most dwarf conifers are in scale with one another, they should be grouped rather than "dotted" around the landscape where they can only be viewed one at a time. Some of the larger dwarf shrubs combine effectively in foundation plantings because they are in scale with the modern house.

Most conifers require full sun to bring out their true beauty. Hemlock and some of the spruce require at least ½ day of full sunlight; *Tsuga canadensis* 'Cole' will thrive on only a few hours of sunshine each day.

Foliage color varies according to the season, temperature, or intensity of sunlight. Shade may reduce the bright yellow or white in the variegated plants, but these colors can usually be restored when the plants are brought into more intense sunlight.

Dwarf conifers should *always* be purchased as balled-and-burlapped or container-grown plants because they live in association with mycorrhiza (fungi that surround the roots and assist the plants in obtaining nutrients from the soil). Since mycorrhiza are more sensitive to sunlight and dry air than the roots, a conifer purchased bare-root may not retain enough mycorrhiza after transplanting to benefit the plant.

Whenever possible, purchase plants that are "growing on their own roots" (plants that have been propagated from cuttings and not grafted onto the rootstock of another species or cultivar). Conifers respond to rootstock vigor in much the same way as apple trees. The scion (top shoot) grafted onto a vigorous rootstock may lose its dwarf character, while the same scion grafted onto a slow-growing rootstock will not. A grafted plant will show a healed scar from the graft on the trunk about 1 inch above the groundline. It is, of course, impossible to determine what rootstock was used.

Pine, hemlock, and some of the spruce are difficult to propagate from cuttings, and are usually grafted. These grafted plants are healthier and live longer than

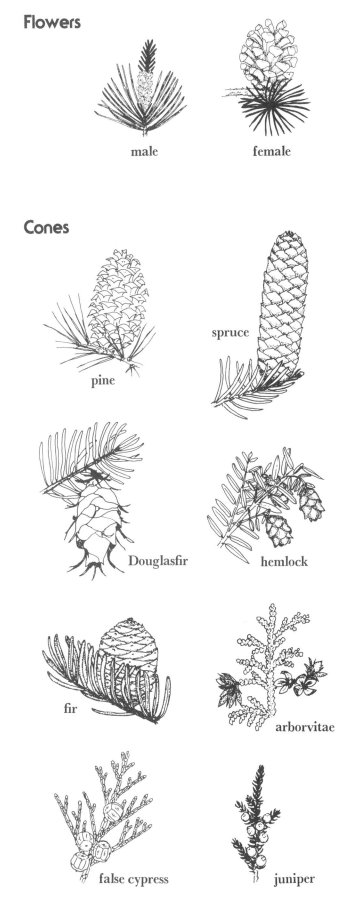

Flowers

male   female

Cones

pine   spruce

Douglasfir   hemlock

fir   arborvitae

false cypress   juniper

Dwarf plant with a strong
sucker growing from the
rootstock.

Dwarf weeping plant that
has reverted to a normal
upright growth habit.

Dwarf plant with 2 branches
that have reverted to the
original large, fast-growing
plant.

if they had been successfully rooted from cuttings.
Few dwarf conifers are reproduced from seed. Seed
propagation usually results in variation among the
seedlings. Plants propagated vegetatively by cuttings or
grafting are a portion of the original plant that is
rooted and usually maintain the characteristics
of that plant.

Most dwarf conifers grow best in a well-drained,
slightly acid, sandy loam soil. If the soil is heavy clay,
prepare the beds by loosening the soil to a depth of
about 1 to 1½ feet; discard about ⅔ of the clay, and
add ⅓ sand and ⅓ peat moss to the remaining clay.
Mix thoroughly and allow the soil to settle for a few
weeks. If the soil is slightly alkaline, plant only junipers
or yews, or grow the plants in raised beds (see
Rhododendron, page 75).

The dwarf conifers have a low fertility requirement,
and may respond by above-normal growth if heavily
fertilized. Nutrients should be provided in the form of
well-decomposed organic matter such as rotted
manure, leafmold, or compost.

Although they are fairly tolerant of dry conditions,
conifers should not be allowed to undergo a prolonged
drouth period. Newly planted conifers should have
supplemental water until they are well established.

Dwarf conifers should be heavily watered in the fall
so that they go into the winter with abundant moisture.
During the winter, they continue to transpire (evaporate moisture through their needles), and are unable
to replace the water lost because the roots are dormant.
Without sufficient moisture, they can desiccate (dry
up) and die during the winter months.

These plants benefit from a year-round mulch.

Dwarf conifers should be pruned to train the
upright plants, to keep the prostrate plants in bounds,
and to remove any branches that have "reverted."
Reversion is the appearance on a dwarf plant of
the characteristic growth of the species from which the
plant was derived. This mutation occurs more often
among plants originating from bud sports than from
those originating from seedlings. The difference in the
branches becomes more obvious after one or more
growing seasons. The growth should be cut out because
it usually destroys the character of the dwarf. In
certain pendulous forms, reversion may result in upright or leader branches that eventually grow strong
and treelike. These branches should be removed as
soon as they are discovered.

Removing rival leaders on the upright plants
prevents overcrowding, and results in a more attractive
plant. Pinching the growing tips of a sparsely
branched plant will encourage denser growth. When
transplanting, carefully remove damaged and unattractive parts and prune to balance the upper portion
of the plant with the root system.

Relatively few pests attack dwarf conifers. The
most common is the two-spotted mite (or red spider
mite) that is too small to be seen with the naked eye.
This pest causes the foliage to appear dull and, if
unchecked, may lead to discoloration of the foliage and
eventual death of the plant.

To determine if two-spotted mites are present, hold
a branch of the plant over a sheet of white paper
and shake the branch. If any specks on the paper
move, the plant is probably infested with two-spotted
mites. Hosing the plant with a forceful spray of water
once a week will usually control these pests. If the
problem persists, you may need to apply a chemical
spray. Spruce and hemlock are especially susceptible
to attacks from two-spotted mites.

The foliage of conifers quickly turns brown from
cat or dog urine. Scorching sun or strong winds can
also cause browning of the leaves of certain cultivars,
especially those with new spring growth. These plants
should be placed in a sheltered site. If the tips of the
foliage are burned, wait until the foliage is completely
shriveled and brown; then vigorously beat, brush, or
shake the plant to cause the dead leaves to drop off.

Shake the plants free of heavy snow as soon as
possible after the snow has ceased to fall, and before
wind, rain, frost, or a combination of these increases
the weight of the snow upon the plants to the point of
damaging the main branches. You may need to tie
the branches of the upright cultivars. Shoveled snow
should never be placed on the branches. Snow becomes
quite heavy as it compacts, and may cause the
branches to break.

Collections of Dwarf Conifers

Dwarf conifers became popular in Europe during the middle of the nineteenth century, and many excellent collections may be found in Europe and the United States. The collections in this country include the following:

Arnold Arboretum
The Arborway
Jamaica Plains, Massachusetts 02130

Bartlett Arboretum of the State of Connecticut
151 Brookdale Road
Stamford, Connecticut 06903

Bernheim Forest Arboretum
Claremont, Kentucky 40110

Austin C. Harper
Moline, Illinois
(private collection)

Hershey Rose Gardens and Arboretum
Hershey, Pennsylvania 17033

Hidden Lake Gardens
Michigan State University
Tipton, Michigan 49287

Longwood Gardens
Kennett Square, Pennsylvania 19348

Morris Arboretum
University of Pennsylvania
9414 Meadowbrook Avenue
Philadelphia, Pennsylvania 19118

New York Botanical Gardens
Bronx Park
Bronx, New York 10458

Strybing Arboretum
Golden Gate Park
9th Avenue and Lincoln Way
San Francisco, California 94122
(collection of James Nobel)

United States National Arboretum
Gotelli Collection
24th and R Streets N. E.
Washington, D.C. 20002

University of Rhode Island
Department of Plant and Soil Science
Kingston, Rhode Island 02881

White Flower Farm
Litchfield, Connecticut 06759
(retail and mail order nursery)

Pinaceae (Pine family)

Zone 4

Compact White Fir

May also be listed as *Abies concolor compacta,*
Abies concolor violacea compacta, Abies concolor var.
glauca 'Compacta'

Abies concolor 'Compacta' is a dense, compact,
flat-topped plant that tends to grow asymmetrically.
Growth rate is slow (1 to 2 inches per year). A 25-
year-old plant measured 2½ feet high and 3½ feet
wide. Texture is medium.

The branches are crowded and upright. The
numerous branchlets are short, stout, stiff, and close
together. They ascend and arch at the tips.

The greyish-blue leaves are either straight or falcate
(sickle-shaped), and are arranged in 2 ranks. They
are stiff, thick, about 1 to 1¾ inches long (slightly
smaller than those of the species), and have 2 faint
lines (stomata) separated by a green band on
the undersides.

The large, broadly conical buds are blunt, and are
covered with a thick resin that conceals the scales.

Abies concolor 'Compacta' grows best in full sun in
deep, rich, moist, well-drained, gravelly or sandy loam
soils, and does not perform well in heavy clay soils.
It tolerates light shade, city conditions, heat,
drouth, and cold. The plant is not seriously affected by
insects or diseases.

It may be used in the foundation planting, rock
garden, or as a specimen plant.

Abies concolor 'Compacta' is one of the most
handsome and distinctive of the dwarf conifers. It was
introduced in 1891.

The *Abies* differ from their nearest relative, *Picea*
(spruce) in leaf-scar characteristics. When the leaves
drop from the branches of the *Abies* species, a disclike
scar is visible; when the leaves drop from *Picea,* a
small, prominent, peglike projection remains.

Pinaceae (Pine family)   Dwarf Korean Fir

Zone 5   May also be listed as *Abies koreana compacta, Abies koreana nana*

Abies koreana 'Compact Dwarf' is a compact, symmetrical, horizontal, bun-shaped plant that does not bear cones and has no central leader. Its ultimate size is 4 feet high and 4 feet wide. Growth rate is slow. Texture is medium.

The leaves of the species are dark green, sharply pointed, rounded or notched at the apexes, ½ to ¾ inch long and $\frac{1}{12}$ to $\frac{1}{16}$ inch wide, grooved on the upper sides, and white, with 2 broad stomatic bands, on the undersides. The leaves of *Abies koreana* 'Compact Dwarf' are similar to those of the species but are somewhat shorter.

Abies koreana 'Compact Dwarf' grows best in full sun in a deep, rich, moist, well-drained, gravelly or sandy loam soil, and does not perform well in heavy clay soils. It tolerates full shade. The plant should not be grown south of Zone 5b.

Abies koreana 'Compact Dwarf' may be used in the foundation planting or as a specimen plant.

The origin of this plant is unknown.

Cupressaceae (Cypress family)

Zone 6

Koster's Hinoki False Cypress

May also be listed as *Chamaecyparis obtusa*
var. *nana kosteri*

Chamaecyparis obtusa 'Kosteri' is an informal,
loosely compact, pyramidal shrub. The plant tends to
be somewhat sprawling, and is best grown with its
central stem trained upward as a leader. The
horizontal branches then spread out in layers, display-
ing the foliage to best advantage. The ultimate size of
this plant is about 3½ feet high and 3 to 4 feet wide.
Growth rate is slow. Texture is fine.

The branchlets are ascending, with downcurving
tips.

The leaves are in lateral pairs and appressed to
the stem, with only the blunt ends free. The large,
bright green fans of lush foliage turn bronze in the
autumn. These mossylike fans are curiously twisted
(one lateral side up and the other down), giving the
plant a distinctive appearance. The layerlike effect can
be accentuated by carefully thinning the foliage.

Chamaecyparis obtusa 'Kosteri' is an intermediate
form between *Chamaecyparis obtusa* 'Nana' and
Chamaecyparis obtusa 'Pygmaea' in both foliage
and growth.

The plant grows best in a moist, well-drained,
neutral or acidic soil and a moderately humid atmosphere in a sunny area protected from the wind.
It suffers from winter burn during severe winters.

Chamaecyparis obtusa 'Kosteri' may be used in
the foundation planting, rock garden, or as a specimen
plant. It is one of the most attractive and popular
of the *Chamaecyparis obtusa* cultivars.

Chamaecyparis obtusa 'Kosteri' was introduced
by the firm of M. Koster and Son, Boskoop, Netherlands. It has been cultivated since 1915.

Cupressaceae (Cypress family)

Zone 6

Lycopodioides Hinoki False Cypress

May also be listed as *Chamaecyparis obtusa* var. *lycopodioides, Retinospora lycopodioides, Chamaecyparis obtusa* var. *lycopodioides* 'Rashahiba'

Chamaecyparis obtusa 'Lycopodioides' is an asymmetrical, sparse, openly branched, globose plant that becomes gaunt with age. Growth rate is slow (usually ½ inch per year). The plant may attain a height of 6 feet and a width of 8 feet in 30 years. Texture is fine.

The main branches are rigid, thick, spreading, and sparse. The coarse, 4-sided branchlets are scattered, irregularly set on the branches, and densely crowded (especially toward the ends of the branches).

The foliage is unique among the *Chamaecyparis obtusa* cultivars. The masses of dark blue-green, mossylike foliage are especially crowded towards the ends of the branches, and may be arranged in many vertical rows. The leaves are elongated, blunt at the apexes, and keeled on the backs. They are variously shaped: the upper leaves are terete (cylindrical) or bluntly awl-shaped and spirally arranged; those near the bases of the principal shoots are scalelike, oval, appressed in opposite pairs, and imbricated (overlapping).

Chamaecyparis obtusa 'Lycopodioides' grows best in a moist, well-drained, neutral or acidic soil and a moderately humid atmosphere in a sunny area protected from the wind. It suffers from winter burn during severe winters. Pruning the branches will encourage the plant to branch out.

It may be used in the foundation planting, rock garden, or as a specimen plant.

Chamaecyparis obtusa 'Lycopodioides' was introduced from Japan in 1861 by Philip van Siebold. Robert Fortune sent the plant to Standish Nurseries, Bagshot, England, about the same time that John G. Vietch introduced it.

Cupressaceae (Cypress family)

Zone 6

Boulevard Sawara False Cypress

May also be listed as *Chamaecyparis pisifera cyanoviridis*

Chamaecyparis pisifera 'Boulevard' quickly forms a neat, bluish gray, dense, broadly pyramidal, symmetrical plant. Growth rate is medium, and this plant may not be a true dwarf. A 20-year-old plant measured 8 feet high. Texture is fine.

The silvery blue-gray leaves are awl-shaped, curving, ¼ to ⅜ inch long, finely pointed but not prickly, narrow, and linear.

Chamaecyparis pisifera 'Boulevard' grows best in a moist, loamy, well-drained, lime-free soil, a humid atmosphere, and a shaded, protected site. The plant develops the best foliage color when grown in the shade. When grown in an exposed site, the leaves turn a bronze color in winter. The foliage fails to develop its true color (becoming a dirty brown) when the plant is grown in soils containing lime. The plant may be maintained at a lower height by pruning. It shows considerable winter injury north of Zone 5b.

One of the most popular dwarf conifers, *Chamaecyparis pisifera* 'Boulevard' may be used in the foundation planting, shrub border, a permanent landscape container, or as a specimen plant. It may grow too large for use in the rock garden.

The plant is easily propagated from cuttings.

Chamaecyparis pisifera 'Boulevard' is a juvenile form that originated as a sport of *Chamaecyparis pisifera* 'Squarrosa' about 1934.

Cupressaceae (Cypress family)

Zone 6

Dwarf Thread Sawara False Cypress

May also be listed as *Chamaecyparis pisifera filifera nana*

Chamaecyparis pisifera 'Filifera Nana' is a compact, dense, rounded, broad, flat-topped shrub. Growth rate is slow. A 10-year-old plant measured 1 foot high and 3 feet wide; a 25-year-old plant measured 2 feet 6 inches high and 3 feet 9 inches wide. Texture is fine.

The branchlets are slender, long, and pendulous.

The dark-green leaves are trailing and threadlike, giving an attractive "weeping" effect.

The plant requires an open site, a moist, loamy, lime-free, well-drained soil, full sun, and a humid atmosphere.

Chamaecyparis pisifera 'Filifera Nana' is quite attractive when used in the foundation planting or among rocks. It is similar to but smaller than its parent, *Chamaecyparis pisifera* 'Filifera'.

This plant was raised in the forestry at Tharandt, Germany, about 1897.

Cupressaceae (Cypress family)

Zone 6

Dwarf Moss Sawara False Cypress

May also be listed as *Chamaecyparis pisifera* var. *squarrosa minima, Chamaecyparis pisifera squarrosa pygmaea, Chamaecyparis pisifera* var. *minima*

Chamaecyparis pisifera 'Squarrosa Minima' is a dense, compact, globular dwarf shrub that forms a spreading, almost prostrate mat when mature. Growth rate is slow (about ½ inch per year). Texture is fine.

The branchlets are crowded and erect, with short sprays.

The silvery blue leaves gradually taper to a point. They are in whorls of 2 or 3, crowded, very thin, and recurve at right angles to the branchlets. The broad, green midrib on the undersides of the leaves is separated by two slightly sunken white lines (stomata).

Chamaecyparis pisifera 'Squarrosa Minima' tends to revert to *Chamaecyparis pisifera* 'Squarrosa Intermedia', and many intermediate forms can be found. The reverted portion should be promptly removed. The plant is similar to *Chamaecyparis obtusa* 'Intermedia', but is slower growing, denser, more dwarfed, and has a neater habit and smaller foliage.

Chamaecyparis pisifera 'Squarrosa Minima' grows best in a moist, loamy, well-drained, lime-free soil. This plant tolerates full sun in the summer, but needs shade in the winter to prevent sunscald. It suffers considerable winter dieback when grown north of Zone 5b.

Chamaecyparis pisifera 'Squarrosa Minima' may be used in the foundation planting, rock garden, or as a specimen plant.

Cupressaceae (Cypress family)

Zone 4

Sargent's Chinese Juniper

May also be listed as *Juniperus procumbens, Juniperus chinensis* var. *procumbens*

Juniperus chinensis var. *sargentii* is a prostrate, matlike shrub that slowly forms a dense carpet. It grows about 1½ to 2 feet high and 8 to 10 feet wide. Growth rate is medium to slow. Texture is medium.

The main branches are stout and prostrate, with short, ascending branchlets. The erect branchlets are 4-angled, and are covered with leaves.

The gray-green leaves are mostly scalelike, small, appressed, lightly grooved on the back, and glaucous. The leaves are in whorls of 3, keeled below and concave above, with a raised midrib. They are closely set and loosely appressed on the branchlets and growing tips, giving them a "cordlike" appearance. The young plants bear acicular (needle-shaped) leaves; the adult plants do not. The leaves smell unpleasantly of camphor when crushed.

The fruits are glaucous blue cones that contain 3 seeds.

This plant adapts readily to soil and site. It seems to be unaffected by *Phomopsis juniperovora* (juniper blight fungus), but is susceptible to cedar apple rust.

It may be used in the foundation planting, on top of a wall, as a ground cover on slopes, in a permanent landscape container, or in an open site (plants spaced 6 to 8 feet apart).

Juniperus chinensis var. *sargentii* is a native of Japan, Korea, the Kuriles, and Sakhalin, where it grows on rocky cliffs and seashores. It was introduced by Professor Sargent of the Arnold Arboretum, Jamaica Plains, Massachusetts, in 1892. Two cultivars are available — *Juniperus sargentii* 'Glauca' (blue form) and *Juniperus sargentii* 'Viridis' (green form).

Cupressaceae (Cypress family)

Zone 6

Shore Juniper

May also be listed as *Juniperus litoralis*

Juniperus conferta is a prostrate, dense, mat-forming shrub that grows 6 inches high and spreads 6 to 9 feet after 10 to 15 years. Growth rate is fast. Texture is fine.

The thick main branches spread over the ground, and are covered with a reddish-brown bark. The greenish-white branchlets are dense and spreading.

The rich, bright apple-green leaves are concave, with a white stomatic band on the upper sides, and convex on the undersides. The leaves are crowded, about ½ inch long, awl-shaped, in whorls of 3, overlapping, and nearly cover the branchlets. Each leaf tapers to a sharp point, and the plant is distinctly prickly to the touch. This characteristic distinguishes *Juniperus conferta* from *Juniperus conferta* var. *maritima* (also known as *Juniperus taxifolia* var. *lutchuensis*), which has long been grown in England.

The abundant fruits are ⅓ to ½ inch in diameter, flat at the base, and a glaucous purplish black at maturity.

Juniperus conferta grows best on a light, sandy soil and in full sun. It suffers winter dieback if grown north of Zone 6b. The plant tolerates pruning. It is extremely susceptible to *Phomopsis juniperovora* (juniper blight fungus) and may be injured by rabbits.

This plant may be used in the foundation planting, shrub border, or as a ground cover in sandy soil, and is one of the few shrubs that will hang downward over a wall or bank. Its foliage contrasts effectively with the dark-green *Juniperus communis* cultivars and the blue and gray cultivars of *Juniperus horizontalis*.

Juniperus conferta has been propagated by seed, but is now more commonly propagated from cuttings.

The plant is native to Japan and Sakhalin, where it grows in sand dunes in coastal areas. It was introduced by Ernest H. Wilson to the Arnold Arboretum, Jamaica Plains, Massachusetts, in 1915.

For a color illustration of **Juniperus conferta**, see page 144.

Cupressaceae (Cypress family)

Zone 4b

Bar Harbor Creeping Juniper

May also be listed as *Juniperus horizontalis* var. *Bar Harbor*

Juniperus horizontalis 'Bar Harbor' is a compact, dense shrub that spreads in all directions, with thin, flexible main stems that easily follow the contours of the ground or weave gracefully between the rocks. The plant grows about 1 foot high and spreads 6 to 8 feet across. Growth rate is fast (up to 15 inches per year). Texture is medium-fine.

The long, thin main branches are prostrate and horizontal or nearly horizontal at the tips. The side branches ascend at varying angles. All branchlets turn upward to produce a V-shaped spray. The bark of the new wood is yellow-brown. The growing tips are mauve.

The leaves are very small, tightly appressed, and scalelike. The foliage is a deep grass green. Since the leaves are heavily coated with a white, glaucous bloom, however, the summer foliage appears to be a grayish-green, with a brown tinge at the tips of the leaves. The foliage becomes mauve after the first frosts, and maintains this color throughout the winter.

The flowers are dioecious (staminate or male and pistillate or female flowers are borne on separate plants), and are inconspicuous.

The slightly glaucous, bluish or greenish-black fruits are cones, about ⅓ inch in diameter, that are borne on recurved stalks. The fruits are seldom produced on cultivated plants.

Juniperus horizontalis 'Bar Harbor' will grow in shallow soil. It requires full sun, and is extremely susceptible to *Phomopsis juniperovora* (juniper blight fungus). This plant can be pruned severely to keep it in bounds.

Juniperus horizontalis 'Bar Harbor' is grown for its lush, deep-piled carpet effect. It may be used in the foundation planting, shrub border, a mass planting, rock garden, a permanent landscape container, as a ground cover, and on a slope. Because the branches tend to drape downward, the plant is excellent for "softening" large rocks.

The name *Juniperus horizontalis* 'Bar Harbor' encompasses a group of plants found growing wild near Bar Harbor on the northeastern side of Mt. Desert Island, Maine. These plants were discovered growing in the crevices on the rocky coast, frequently within range of the salt spray. Several clones are in cultivation in England and many in the United States.

For a general discussion of **Juniperus horizontalis** cultivars, see page 106.

Cupressaceae (Cypress family)

Zone 4b

Wilton's Creeping Juniper

May also be listed as *Juniperus horizontalis* 'Blue Wiltoni', *Juniperus horizontalis* 'Wilton Carpet', *Juniperus horizontalis* 'Blue Rug'

Juniperus horizontalis 'Wiltonii' is a dense, completely prostrate shrub with trailing branches. It rarely attains a height of 6 inches but spreads to 4 to 5 feet wide. Growth rate is slow. Texture is fine.

The long, slender branches are prostrate, and form flat, glaucous-blue carpets.

The small, rich silvery blue leaves are closely appressed. They retain their color throughout the winter.

The inconspicuous flowers are dioecious (staminate or male and pistillate or female flowers are borne on separate plants).

The bright blue fruits are cones, about ⅓ inch in diameter, that are borne on recurved stalks.

The plant is moderately susceptible to *Phomopsis juniperovora* (juniper blight fungus).

Juniperus horizontalis 'Wiltonii' is the slowest growing, most prostrate, and one of the most popular of the blue cultivars of *Juniperus horizontalis*. It is grown for its rich blue foliage and blue fruits.

This plant may be used in a permanent landscape container or over gravel or flagstones. It should not be used where it will be in competition with grass and other plants.

It is sold under the names 'Blue Wilton', 'Glauca Wiltonii', 'Blue Rug', 'Wilton Carpet' (Wilton is a well-known brand of carpet in England), 'Glauca', and 'Glauca Nana'.

Juniperus horizontalis 'Wiltonii' was discovered in 1914 by J. C. van Heiningen of the South Wilton Nurseries, South Wilton, Connecticut, on Vinalhaven Island, Maine.

General Discussion of *Juniperus horizontalis* cultivars

There are many other prostrate forms of *Juniperus horizontalis*. These plants grow best in open, sunny locations and light, sandy, moderately moist soils. They tolerate hot, dry sites and heavy or rocky soils, but do not grow well in dense shade, becoming thin, open, and scraggly. *Juniperus horizontalis* cultivars can be pruned, and are tolerant of air pollution and city conditions. These cultivars vary considerably in their susceptibility to *Phomopsis juniperovora* (juniper blight fungus).

Juniperus horizontalis cultivars may be used in the foundation planting, shrub borders, mass plantings, permanent landscape containers, to cover slopes, and as low ground covers.

Cupressaceae (Cypress family)

Zone 4

Japgarden Juniper (American),
Creeping Juniper (Great Britain)

May also be listed as *Juniperus chinensis* var.
procumbens

Juniperus procumbens is a spreading, prostrate, dwarf shrub with long, stiff branches that form a dense, rigid, thick mat. It can grow 1 to 2 feet high in the center and spread 10 to 15 feet wide. Growth rate is medium. Texture is medium.

The stout, stiff branches turn up at the tips. They are spreading, closely packed in the center of the plant, and grow radially. The branchlets have glaucous ridges.

The sharply pointed leaves are ¼ to ⅓ inch long, awl-shaped, linear, in whorls of 3, and crowded on the branchlets. The upper sides are concave and glaucous, with a green midrib. The undersides are convex, bluish, and have 2 white spots near the base from which 2 glaucous lines run down a ridge (actually the lower part of the leaf uniting it to the stem). The bluish-green color is maintained throughout the year.

The flowers are dioecious (staminate or male and pistillate or female flowers are borne on separate plants). The staminate flowers are yellow and the pistillate flowers are greenish.

The fruits are about ⅓ inch in diameter, and contain 2 to 3 seeds. They seldom appear on cultivated plants.

Juniperus procumbens will grow in moist soils, but needs full sun and an open, well-drained site. Because it is difficult to transplant, you should purchase balled-and-burlapped or container-grown plants. The plant tolerates heavy pruning and can be trained to grow upward. It is slightly susceptible to *Phomopsis juniperovora* (juniper blight fungus), and is subject to attack from the two-spotted mite.

Juniperus procumbens may be used in the shrub border, on the terrace, and as a ground cover on hillsides or banks in "naturalized" areas. Because of its uneven growth, it is not suitable for use as a ground cover in a focal point of the lawn that is viewed at close range. Single plants are excellent in the rock garden.

The plant roots freely from cuttings.

Juniperus procumbens is closely related to *Juniperus squamata,* but has longer, stiffer leaves and glaucous shoots.

Although originally discovered growing wild on the mountains and seashores of Japan, *Juniperus procumbens* has not been found in these areas in recent years. It is a popular plant in Japanese gardens.

The plant was named *Juniperus procumbens* by Philip von Siebold in 1844, and was exhibited by him in the Netherlands in 1850. It was not widely established in European cultivation at that time, however, and was reintroduced by Maurice L. de Vilmorin into France as *Juniperus japonica* in 1903.

Cupressaceae (Cypress family)

Zone 4

Dwarf Japgarden Juniper

May also be listed as *Juniperus procumbens* var. *nana*, *Juniperus japonica* 'Nana', *Juniperus squamata* var. *prostrata*

Juniperus procumbens 'Nana' forms a dense, compact mat with branches on top of one another. It is smaller and slower growing than *Juniperus procumbens*. A 10-year-old plant measured 1 foot high and 4 feet wide. Texture is fine.

The branches are shorter and the stems are thicker than those of the species. The branchlets vary in length, spreading out as compact masses of sprays.

The leaves are shorter and wider than those of *Juniperus procumbens*. They are small, rigid, closely set, and awl-shaped. The new spring growth is bright green, becoming bluish green in the summer and slightly purplish in the winter.

Juniperus procumbens 'Nana' has the same cultural requirements as the species. It is moderately susceptible to *Phomopsis juniperovora* (juniper blight fungus). The plant can be allowed to grow naturally, or the leader can be staked upright as a trunk and the branches trained horizontally to hold a "tree top" of miniature foliage.

It may be used wherever space is limited, and in the foundation planting, rock garden, as a specimen plant, ground cover, or as a cascading plant that trails downward over rocks and tree roots.

Juniperus procumbens 'Nana' was introduced from Japan by D. Hill Nursery, Dundee, Illinois, in 1922.

For a color illustration of **Juniperus procumbens** 'Nana', see page 144.

Pinaceae (Pine family)

Zone 3

Gregory's Dwarf Norway Spruce

May also be listed as *Picea abies* var. *gregoryana, Abies excelsa gregoryana*

Picea abies 'Gregoryana' is one of the most popular dwarf cultivars of *Picea abies*. The young plant has a dense, bun-shaped to globose (spherical) habit similar to *Picea abies* 'Echiniformis'. As the plant matures, however, it opens up into billowy, globose masses. This tendency can be reduced by careful annual pruning. The plant rarely exceeds 2 feet in height. Growth rate is very slow. A 30-year-old plant measured 1½ feet high and 3½ feet wide. Texture is medium.

The branches are quite short and compact. The white or grayish brown branchlets are crowded, thin, slightly drooping and hairy, and point forward.

The radially arranged leaves are ¼ to ½ inch long, mostly pointed forward in tufts, roundish, straight, with 1, 2, or 3 stomatic lines on each side, and taper abruptly. The uppermost leaves on the shoot appear in a starlike circle at the base of the terminal cluster, exposing the buds. Because of the dense growth, the leaves interlock with leaves from adjoining shoots, forming an impenetrable mass.

The buds are minute and globose, with pale yellow-green tips that are not covered with scales.

The winter buds are conspicuous, globose or egg-shaped. The terminal buds, varying in number up to 10 or more, are surrounded by a ring of dark-brown scales. There are 1 or 2 lateral buds at the bases of the strongest shoots.

Picea abies 'Gregoryana' should be grown in full sun in a moderately moist, sandy, well-drained soil. It needs supplemental watering, especially during the first few years after planting. Although the plant performs best north of Zone 4, it can be grown successfully as far south as Zone 6a if planted in a cool site and kept moist during the growing season. It is subject to attack from the two-spotted mite.

This plant may be used in the foundation planting or as a specimen plant.

Picea abies 'Gregoryana' was first grown in Gregory's Royal Nurseries in Cirencester Nurseries, England, about 1850.

Pinaceae (Pine family)

Zone 3

Maxwell's Norway Spruce

May also be listed as *Picea abies* var. *maxwellii*, *Abies excelsa maxwellii*, *Picea excelsa maxwellii*, *Picea abies* var. *pseudomaxwellii*, *Picea excelsa* var. *pseudomaxwellii*

Picea abies 'Maxwellii' is a compact, rounded, flat-domed, asymmetrical shrub with a mass of stout, short branchlets. Growth rate is slow. A 38-year-old plant measured 3½ feet high and 10 feet wide. Texture is medium.

The branches are short and stiff. The white or yellowish-brown branchlets are mostly ascending, spreading, short, and thick.

The bright, sea-green leaves are coarse, rigid, roundish, and slightly curved, with 3 stomatic lines on each side. They are ⅓ to ½ inch long, and are narrower at the upper ⅓, tapering abruptly to a long, very fine, hairlike point that is sometimes hooked. The leaves are radial on the upright branchlets, pointing out and slightly forward, and are not set close together. The leaves on the lower branchlets are imperfectly radial.

The winter buds are egg-shaped, thick, moderately blunt, stout, and dark brown with lighter centers.

Picea abies 'Maxwellii' should be grown in full sun in a moderately moist, sandy, well-drained soil. It needs supplemental watering, especially during the first few years after planting. Although the plant performs best north of Zone 4, it can be grown successfully as far south as Zone 6a if planted in a cool site and kept moist during the growing season. It is susceptible to attack from the two-spotted mite.

This plant may be used in the foundation planting, rock garden, or as a specimen plant.

Picea abies 'Maxwellii' originated in Geneva, New York, on the grounds of T. E. Maxwell Brothers, and was named in Europe in 1874. It is widely grown in the United States and Europe. The cultivars grown in Europe are more compact than those grown in the United States.

Pinaceae (Pine family)

Zone 3

Sharpleaf Norway Spruce

May also be listed as *Picea abies mucronata, Abies excelsa* var. *mucronata, Picea excelsa mucronata*

Picea abies 'Mucronata' is a dense, robust, broadly pyramidal conifer with uniform growth. It is characterized by curved main branches and numerous large buds. This plant is a dwarf form until it is about 15 years old, and can eventually reach 15 to 30 feet in height. Growth rate is medium. Texture is medium.

The main branches rise at a 60-degree (occasionally 90-degree) angle, and bear the leaves radially. The branches and branchlets are yellowish brown. The larger branches are unusually stout and thick, often growing erect at the tips. The branchlets are very crowded. The light orange-brown shoots are glossy, thick, and stiff.

The glossy, dark blue-green leaves are radially arranged, and are pectinate (microscopic glassy hooks in a row resembling the teeth of a comb). They are ¼ to ⅝ inch long, uniformly wide, thick, and flat, with a slight upward curve at the tip, ending abruptly in a fine, sharp point. There are 3 rows of stomatic lines on both sides that do not extend to the tip.

The bright orange-brown winter buds are thick, bluntly pointed, and round. A single terminal bud and many lateral buds are borne.

Picea abies 'Mucronata' should be grown in full sun in a moderately moist, sandy, well-drained soil. It needs supplemental watering, especially during the first few years after planting. Although the plant performs best north of Zone 4, it can be grown successfully as far south as Zone 6a if planted in a cool site and kept moist during the growing season. It is subject to attack from the two-spotted mite.

This plant may be used in the foundation planting, rock garden, or as a specimen plant.

Picea abies 'Mucronata' was discovered by the chief horticulturist of the Trianon Gardens, Versailles, France, about 1835.

Pinaceae (Pine family)

Zone 3

Birdsnest Norway Spruce

May also be listed as *Picea abies midiformis, Picea excelsa nidiformis*

Picea abies 'Nidiformis' is a dense, rounded, symmetrical, flat-topped, broad shrub. It is spreading to prostrate in form. Growth rate is slow. A 10-year-old plant measured 1 foot high and 2 feet 4 inches wide, and a 30-year-old plant measured 2 feet high and 6 feet wide. Texture is medium.

The main branches are ascending, very crowded, and form a series of tight, horizontal layers with gracefully outward-curving tips. The glossy, light, whitish-brown branchlets are crowded, spreading, thin, flexible, and are directed forward and upward.

The dark, dull, greenish-gray leaves are flat, thin, narrow, slightly curved, and about ⅜ inch long. The apex tapers abruptly to a slightly incurved, cartilaginous point. There are 1 to 2 stomatic lines on each side. The leaves are few on the upper sides of the branchlets, and point forward and slightly upward; the lower ranks point out or slightly forward. The lower edges of the leaves are pectinate (microscopic glassy hooks in a row resembling the teeth of a comb). The leaves are especially attractive in the spring when the buds burst into a bright, fresh green growth that is somewhat pendulous at first and becomes straighter as the wood hardens.

The dark-brown winter buds are inconspicuous, ⅛ inch long, conical, and bluntly pointed. The terminal bud is longer than the lateral buds, and is usually solitary.

Picea abies 'Nidiformis' should be grown in full sun in a moderately moist, sandy, well-drained soil. It needs supplemental watering, especially during the first few years after planting. Although the plant performs best north of Zone 4, it can be grown successfully as far south as Zone 6a if planted in a cool site and kept moist during the growing season. The young branchlets develop in early spring, and can be injured by frost. The plant is subject to attack from the two-spotted mite.

Picea abies 'Nidiformis' is one of the most common and reliable dwarf cultivars of *Picea abies*. It may be used in the foundation planting, a permanent landscape container, or as a specimen plant.

The plant received its name "Birdsnest Norway Spruce" because of the manner in which the semierect main branches curve outwards and away from the center of the plant, leaving a depression that (especially in younger plants) resembles a large, green bird's nest. Older plants tend to lose this characteristic.

Picea abies 'Nidiformis' was grown by Rulemann Grisson, nurseryman at Sasselheide near Hamburg, Germany, about 1907.

Pinaceae (Pine family)

Zone 3

Pumila Norway Spruce

May also be listed as *Picea abies* var. *pumila*, *Abies excelsa pumila*, *Picea excelsa* var. *pumila*

Picea abies 'Pumila' is a soft, flat-topped, broadly spreading, compact shrub with an irregular outline. The ultimate height of the plant is usually 3 to 4 feet. Growth rate is slow. A 30-year-old specimen measured 2 feet high and 5 feet wide. Texture is medium.

The branches and branchlets are borne in dense, stratified layers. The branches are thick, stiff, and reddish brown. The upper branches are nearly erect, forming a series of layers; the lower ones are wide-spreading and procumbent. The light to reddish-brown branchlets are stout, dense, regularly set at right angles or directed slightly forward, flexible, and with slightly drooping tips. The shoots are medium yellow-brown on the upper sides and medium yellow on the under-sides, and are smooth, thin, and flexible.

The rich, bright green leaves are uniform, thin, soft, flexible, glossy, about ⅜ inch long, and taper from the lower ⅓ to a blunt point. The undersides of the leaves are pectinate (microscopic glossy hooks in a row resembling the teeth of a comb). The leaves are borne semiradially, and lie in distinct ranks or rows. The leaves in each rank are shorter and point more nearly forward than those in the rank below it. The leaves in the upper ranks are crowded and almost hide the branchlets, pointing forward and slightly upward; those in the lower ranks point out and slightly forward.

The dull, light reddish-brown buds are incon-spicuous, pointed, and 1/12 inch long. The solitary terminal bud is subtended by 2 lateral (horizontal) buds.

Picea abies 'Pumila' should be grown in full sun in a moderately moist, sandy, well-drained soil. It needs supplemental moisture, especially during the first few years after planting. Although the plant performs best north of Zone 4, it can be grown successfully as far south as Zone 6a if planted in a cool site and kept moist during the growing season. It is subject to attack from the two-spotted mite.

This plant may be used in the foundation planting or as a specimen plant.

Picea abies 'Pumila Nigra' is similar to *Picea abies* 'Pumila' except that it has darker foliage.

Picea abies 'Pumila' was cultivated in Europe in 1874.

Pinaceae (Pine family)

Zone 5b

Dwarf Alberta White Spruce

May also be listed as *Picea glauca* var. *albertiana conica, Picea albertiana conica, Picea glauca* var. *conica*

Picea glauca 'Conica' is a dense, compact, cone-shaped shrub. Growth rate is slow. A 10-year-old plant measured 2½ feet high and 1 foot wide at the base; a 30-year-old plant measured 5 feet high and 3 feet wide at the base. The plant can eventually grow to a height of 10 feet. Texture is fine.

The branches are erect and flexible. The branchlets are densely set, thin, flexible, and slightly hairy. The new growth is yellowish green, and is covered with a blue-gray bloom that disappears as the shoot matures.

The bright grass-green leaves radiate around the stem, and are thin, ½ inch long, soft, nearly round, more or less curved, of uniform width, and are not set close together. They are grooved, parallel, and taper to a fine cartilaginous point that is not sharp. Each side of the leaf has 1 row of stomatic lines that do not extend to the tip. Fewer leaves radiate from the lower part of the stem, and curve upward toward the light. The foliage is aromatic when crushed.

The light-brown buds are inconspicuous, minute, cylindrical with a rounded tip, slightly resinous except in winter, and are usually borne 3 in a terminal cluster. The strong shoots may have numerous lateral buds.

Picea glauca 'Conica' grows best in a moist, sheltered site. It may suffer from wind scorch and frost during severe winter weather, and is subject to attack from the two-spotted mite. The plant may be maintained at a lower height by annual pruning. Rival leaders should be removed.

Picea glauca 'Conica' may be used in the rock garden, a permanent landscape container, or as a specimen plant.

It is easily propagated by late summer cuttings.

Dr. J. G. Jack and Professor Alfred Rehder discovered this plant growing wild in the Canadian Rockies near Lake Laggan, Alberta, Canada, in 1904. The two men were waiting for a train to return to the Arnold Arboretum after a botanical expedition.

When the train was several hours late, they wandered into a nearby woods, where they found 4 dwarf seedlings that they immediately dug to take back to the Arnold Arboretum. These plants were dwarf varieties of *Picea glauca,* and were named *Picea glauca* 'Conica' by Professor Rehder. The plants were easily propagated, and have since been dispersed throughout the world. The parent tree remains in the Arnold Arboretum. The plant was introduced to the Royal Botanic Gardens, Kew, England, in 1909.

Pinaceae (Pine family)

Zone 5

Dwarf Black Spruce

May also be listed as *Picea mariana nana*, *Picea nigra* var. *nana*

Picea mariana 'Nana' is a dense, compact, globe-shaped plant. Growth rate is very slow. A 15-year-old plant measured 9 inches high and 12 inches wide. Texture is medium.

The branches radiate from the center of the plant. The medium-brown shoots are hairy, thin, and flexible.

The dark, dull, blue-green leaves are short, straight, flexible, round, parallel, and taper to a long point that is not sharp. Numerous large, white stomatic bands are borne in 2 to 4 rows on both sides of the leaf, giving the plant a blue-gray appearance. The foliage is borne radially to the branch.

The medium-brown buds are prominent, globose, dull, and are not resinous. The terminal bud is usually borne singly or with an adjacent smaller bud.

This plant is a dwarf selection from *Picea mariana*, a northern species, and grows best on a moist, well-drained, alluvial bottom soil. It is somewhat susceptible to blight.

Picea mariana 'Nana' may be used in the foundation planting, rock garden, or as a specimen plant. Because of its small size, this plant should be placed where it will be protected from foot traffic, pets, etc.

Picea mariana 'Nana' was first cultivated in 1884.

Pinaceae (Pine family)

Zone 4

Dwarf Serbian Spruce

May also be listed as *Picea omorika* var. *nana*

Picea omorika 'Nana' is a dense, compact, globose-to-conical shrub with attractive foliage. This picturesque plant has a few strongly growing side branches, giving it an irregular form. Its ultimate size is about 4½ feet high and 4 to 6 feet wide. Growth rate is slow. Texture is medium.

The branches are horizontally spreading. The yellow-brown branchlets are densely set, stout, short, and pubescent (hairy). The dull light-brown shoots are thick and quite pubescent.

The widely set leaves radiate around the stem, and are ⅜ inch long, linear, and bluntly pointed. The upper sides are yellow-green, without stomata, and slightly convex. The undersides have up to 7 closely packed, whitish-blue stomata in each of 2 broad bands. The leaves twist, showing both surfaces and giving an attractive glaucous appearance to the plant. The new growth on the tips of the branches is a paler color than the old growth.

The winter buds are dull medium-brown, inconspicuous, long, bluntly pointed, and resinous. The terminal buds are slightly longer than the lateral buds, and are borne 3 to 5 in a cluster. Lateral buds are infrequently borne.

Picea omorika 'Nana' grows best in a deep, rich, moist, well-drained soil, in partial shade, with a dry atmosphere and protected from winter winds. This plant will grow on limestone and acid peats. It is tolerant of city conditions.

Picea omorika 'Nana' is a true dwarf. It may be used in a permanent landscape container or as a specimen plant.

This plant originated as a sport in the nursery of Goudkade Brothers, Boskoop, Netherlands, about 1930.

Pinaceae (Pine family)

Zone 2

Globe Colorado Spruce

May also be listed as *Picea pungens globosa*, *Picea pungens glauca nana*, *Picea pungens* 'Glauca Globosa'

Picea pungens 'Globosa' is a compact, flat-topped, globular, asymmetrical shrub. Growth rate is slow. A 10-year-old plant measured 1 foot 8 inches high and 2 feet 4 inches wide. The ultimate height is about 3 feet. Texture is medium.

The light yellowish-brown branchlets are thin and closely set.

The handsome blue-green leaves are crowded, slightly sickle-shaped, with 3 to 4 stomatic lines on each side, and radiate imperfectly around the stem.

The light-brown buds are egg-shaped and pointed at the tip.

This plant grows best in a rich, moist soil in full sun, and is tolerant of drouth. It can suffer considerable damage from mites, especially in warmer areas.

Picea pungens 'Globosa' may be used in the foundation planting, rock garden, a permanent landscape container, or as a specimen plant.

The plant was grown from seed by Anth. Kluys in Boskoop, Netherlands, in 1937, and was first distributed in 1955 by LeFeber and Company, Boskoop. It is similar to *Picea pungens* 'R.H. Montgomery'.

For a color illustration of **Picea pungens** 'Globosa', see page 144.

Pinaceae (Pine family)

Zone 4

Prostrate Japanese Red Pine

Pinus densiflora 'Prostrata' is a prostrate dwarf conifer. Its main trunk bends over, and the branches follow the contours of the ground. Growth rate is slow. A 20-year-old plant measured 1 foot high and 5 feet wide. Texture is coarse.

The green leaves are 3 inches long, and are borne 2 in a cluster.

No cones have been observed on this cultivar.

This plant grows best in a well-drained, slightly acid soil and a sunny site.

Pinus densiflora 'Prostrata' is a lovely evergreen specimen plant, especially suitable for use in the rock garden or in a permanent landscape container.

Pinaceae (Pine family)   Hill's Mugo Pine

Zone 2   May also be listed as *Pinus mugo compacta,*
                                                        Pinus montana compacta

Pinus mugo 'Compacta' is a dense, almost globose-shaped dwarf shrub. Growth rate is medium. A 40-year-old plant measured 4 feet high and 5 feet wide. Texture is coarse.

The branches ascend, and are more or less erect at the ends.

The slender, bright, dark-green leaves are crowded on the branches, 1 to 1¼ inches long, and are borne 2 to a cluster.

No cones have been observed on this cultivar.

Pinus mugo 'Compacta' grows best in a deep, moist loam in sun or partial shade. This plant tolerates pruning. It is sometimes seriously infested with scale, and is subject to attack from the pine shoot moth.

The plant may be used in the foundation planting, a mass planting, in groupings, in the rock garden, and in a permanent landscape container.

Pinus mugo 'Compacta' originated in the D. Hill Nursery, Dundee, Illinois, about 1923.

Pinus mugo 'Mops' (may also be listed as *Pinus montana mughus* 'Mops') is a slow-growing, bun-shaped dwarf conifer. It is perhaps the most dense cultivar of *Pinus mugo*. A 10-year-old plant measured 1 foot 3 inches high and 2 feet across. The branches are short. The nearly straight leaves taper, and are ¾

to 1¾ inches long and ¹⁄₁₆ inch wide. The winter buds are crowded, brown, and resinous. This plant was selected and propagated by Hugo F. Hooftman, Boskoop, Netherlands, in the late 1940's.

The nomenclature of *Pinus mugo* cultivars is quite confused. Many cultivars are incorrectly labeled, and may not be uniform in size or growth habit.

Pinaceae (Pine family)

Zone 2

Little Mugo Pine

May also be listed as *Pinus pumilio, Pinus montana* var. *pumilio*

Pinus mugo var. *pumilio* is a compact, uniformly rounded, bun-shaped or prostrate, broad shrub, and occasionally has several leaders. It may eventually become 6 feet high and (rarely) 9 feet wide. Growth rate is medium. Texture is coarse.

The branches are thin and prostrate. The branchlets are erect.

The short, rich green leaves are of varying lengths, erect, borne 2 to a cluster, and are spreading near the buds.

The winter buds are very conspicuous.

The cones are sparsely borne on 1 or more older branches. They are sessile (not on a stalk) or very short-stalked, uniform in size, globular, blunt-tipped, and are held erect until maturity. After opening, the cones become horizontal or curve outward. The violet-purple cones darken to a yellow-brown in the autumn.

Pinus mugo var. *pumilio* grows best in a deep, moist, loamy soil in sun or partial shade. The plant tolerates pruning. It may become seriously infested with scale, and is subject to attack from the pine shoot moth.

Pinus mugo var. *pumilio* may be used in the foundation planting, a mass planting, group planting, rock garden, or in a permanent landscape container.

The plant is widely distributed in the Alps of central Europe, and has been known since 1791. *Pinus mugo* var. *pumilio* is often mistakenly sold as *Pinus pumila*.

Pinaceae (Pine family)

Zone 4

Hornibrook Austrian Pine

May also be listed as *Pinus nigra hornibrookiana*

Pinus nigra 'Hornibrookiana' is a small, compact, spreading, ground-hugging shrub. Growth rate is slow. A 10-year-old plant measured 1 foot 3 inches high and 3 feet wide; and a 30-year-old plant measured 2 feet high and 6 feet wide. Texture is coarse.

The strong, stout branches are ascending or erect. The branchlets are stiff. The plant is most attractive during the spring, with its new crop of cream-colored young shoots standing vertically like candles on a cake.

The rich, glossy, black-green leaves are crowded, stiff, straight, sharp-pointed, 2 to 2¼ inches long, and are borne 2 to a cluster.

No cones have been observed on this cultivar.

Pinus nigra 'Hornibrookiana' is tolerant of moist or sandy soils, heat, and drouth. It is extremely susceptible to diplodia tip blight, a fungus that kills the current year's needles and may kill entire shoots.

Pinus nigra 'Hornibrookiana' is one of the few dwarf cultivars of *Pinus nigra*. It may be used in the foundation planting, a permanent landscape container, around rocks, and as a specimen plant.

It is usually propagated by grafting.

H. B. Slavin propagated this plant from a witches'-broom (see pages 3-4) on *Pinus nigra* in Seneca Park, Rochester, New York, about 1930. Slavin named the plant after Murray Hornibrook, plantsman and author of *Dwarf and Slow-Growing Conifers*.

Pinaceae (Pine family)

Zone 3

Japanese Stone Pine (American),
Dwarf Siberian Pine (British, German)

May also be listed as *Pinus cembra* var. *pumila,*
Pinus cembra nana

Pinus pumila varies in habit. It is usually a dwarf with dense, spreading growth, but after many years may exceed 4 feet in height. Growth rate is medium. A 10-year-old plant measured 2 feet high. Texture is coarse.

The grayish-brown branches are crowded, short, and stout. The branchlets are stout, green, and covered with a reddish-brown pubescence (hairiness) the first year, later becoming reddish to grayish brown.

The glaucous, green leaves are densely bundled in clusters of 5, slightly curved, 1½ to 2 inches long, directed forward, and are crowded on the branchlets. The apex is blunt, the margin widely toothed, the outer surface lacks stomata, and the inner surface is glaucous, with 5 to 6 conspicuous stomatic lines. The leaf sheaths drop after the first year.

The reddish-brown winter buds are narrowly conical, ¼ inch long, sharply pointed, and resinous, with blunt apexes and closely pressed scales.

The tiny cones are clustered, short-stalked, 2 inches long, and remain unopened until the seeds are shed. They are violet-purple when they first appear, turn partly green to purple during the second year, and become dull reddish- or yellowish-brown when mature.

Pinus pumila prefers a deep, moist loam in sun or partial shade, and tolerates pruning.

It may be used in the foundation planting, a permanent landscape container, or as a specimen plant.

This plant is generally considered a botanical form of the *Pinus cembra,* but it is usually more prostrate and smaller.

Pinus pumila may be found in large grooves in the mountains of Japan and east Asia, usually in the highest, most exposed sites on windswept plateaus or near the snowline. The plant was introduced into Great Britain in 1807.

Pinaceae (Pine family)

Zone 4

Dwarf Eastern White Pine

May also be listed as *Pinus strobus* var. *nana*, *Pinus strobus* var. *umbraculifera*, *Pinus strobus* var. *pumila*, *Pinus strobus* var. *tabuliformis**

Pinus strobus 'Nana' is a compact, dense, asymmetrical, flat-topped dome-shaped shrub. Its ultimate size is 2 to 3 feet high and 2 to 3 feet wide. Growth rate is slow. Texture is coarse.

The deep-green leaves are soft, 1 to 1½ inches long, with 5 to a cluster arranged so closely as to hide completely the inner branch structure.

No cones have been observed on this cultivar.

Pinus strobus 'Nana' grows best in a fertile, moist, well-drained soil and in full sun to light shade. The plant is very susceptible to sweeping winds, and cannot tolerate air pollutants (ozone, sulfur dioxide) or salts. It is susceptible to white pine blister rust (a bark fungus), and is subject to attack from the white pine weevil.

This plant may be used in the foundation planting, a mass planting, rock garden, or as a specimen plant.

Pinus strobus 'Nana' is intermediate in form between *Pinus strobus* 'Umbraculifera' and *Pinus strobus* 'Prostrata'. There are several forms of this plant. Some are more vigorous and larger growing than others. Certain plants called *Pinus strobus* 'Nana' may actually be *Pinus strobus* 'Radiata'.

---

* Citation according to Murray Hornibrook, *Dwarf and Slow-Growing Conifers* (New York: Charles Scribner's Sons, 1938).

Pinaceae (Pine family)

Zone 4

Umbrella Eastern White Pine

May also be listed as *Pinus strobus umbraculifera, Pinus strobus nana*

Pinus strobus 'Umbraculifera' is a broad, umbrella-shaped dwarf shrub. At maturity, it is vase-shaped, with a round, umbrellalike crown of crowded, slender branchlets and drooping needles. The plant usually reaches about 3 feet in height, rarely exceeding 6 feet. Growth rate is slow. Texture is coarse.

The branches are short and slender, and the reddish-brown branchlets are crowded and glabrous (smooth).

The drooping, light-green leaves are narrow, fine, flexible, 4 inches long, drooping, and in dense clusters (5 leaves to a cluster), with sharp-pointed and serrulate (finely toothed) margins. Occasionally some leaves appear at the summit of a cluster that are only about ½ the length of the other leaves. The leaf sheath is about ¼ inch long, and has a distinct pubescence (hairiness) at its base. The leaf clusters are drooping.

The winter buds are about ⅛ inch long, ovoid, and tapering, with a long point.

Abnormally small cones resembling the species are rarely borne. The resinous cones of *Pinus strobus* are pendant, long-stalked, terete (cylindrical), and often slightly curved. They mature during the second autumn, and remain on the tree long after shedding their seeds.

Pinus strobus 'Umbraculifera' grows best on a fertile, moist, well-drained soil in full sun to light shade. It is susceptible to damage from sweeping winds, and cannot tolerate air pollutants (ozone, sulfur dioxide) or salts. It is susceptible to white pine blister rust (a bark fungus), and is subject to attack from the white pine weevil.

This plant may be used in the foundation planting, rock garden, or as a specimen plant.

Pinus strobus 'Umbraculifera' has been known since 1855. *Pinus strobus* 'Compacta' and *Pinus strobus* 'Densa' are similar to *Pinus stroba* 'Umbraculifera'.

Pinaceae (Pine family)

Zone 2

Dwarf Scotch Pine

May also be listed as *Pinus sylvestris nana,*
Pinus sylvestris pygmaea

Pinus sylvestris 'Nana' is a small, bushy dwarf conifer that rarely reaches 2 feet in height. Growth rate is slow. A 20-year-old plant measured 1 foot 9 inches high and 3 feet wide. Texture is coarse.

The numerous branches are very short, upright, thin, and dense.

The glaucous, green leaves are distinct, straight, and about 1 inch long. They are borne 2 needles to a cluster, and are set far apart.

The buds are not resinous.

No cones have been observed on this cultivar.

This plant grows best in a well-drained, acid soil and full sun, but will grow on poor, dry soils.

Pinus sylvestris 'Nana' is occasionally confused with *Pinus sylvestris* 'Beuvronensis', but it is usually less dense and has nonresinous winter buds.

It may be used in the foundation planting, rock garden, a permanent landscape container, or as a specimen plant.

Pinus sylvestris 'Nana' was introduced about 1855.

Pinaceae (Pine family)

Zone 6

Fletcher's Douglasfir

May also be listed as *Pseudotsuga menziesii fletcheri, Pseudotsuga douglasii* var. *fletcheri, Pseudotsuga glauca* var. *fletcheri*

Pseudotsuga menziesii 'Fletcheri' is a compact, asymmetrical, rounded or flat-topped shrub. Growth rate is slow. A 25-year-old plant at the Royal Horticultural Gardens, Wisly, England, was 4¼ feet high. Texture is medium.

The branches and branchlets are spreading. The gray-brown branchlets are smooth and shining, with occasional short, scattered pubescence (hairiness).

The blue-green leaves are pointed, narrow, ½ to ¾ inch long, curved, and are loosely and nearly radially arranged. The undersides are 2-keeled, and have glaucous bands of stomates; the upper sides are green, with a sunken midrib. The foliage is soft to the touch.

The reddish-brown buds are ¼ inch long, narrow, conical, and finely pointed.

Pseudotsuga menziesii 'Fletcheri' grows best in a neutral or slightly acid, well-drained, moist soil, with full sun and high humidity. It does not tolerate poor, dry soils.

This picturesque shrub is probably the most popular dwarf *Pseudotsuga*. It may be used in the foundation planting, a permanent landscape container, or as a specimen plant.

In his book *Dwarf and Slow-Growing Conifers*, Murray Hornibrook recounts the history of this plant. Lock King Nursery, Weybridge, Surrey, England, had discarded 3 seedlings of *Pseudotsuga glauca* that did not appear to be growing. These seedlings were retrieved by the foreman, who continued to grow them. One seedling had glaucous foliage; the other 2 were more compact and had greener foliage. Mr. Astley, manager of Messrs. Fletcher's Nursery, purchased the glaucous form and 1 of the green forms. He propagated and sold both forms as *Pseudotsuga douglasii* 'Fletcheri'.

Cupressaceae (Cypress family)

Zone 5

Hetz's Midget Eastern Arborvitae

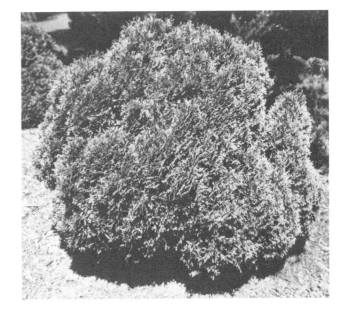

Thuja occidentalis 'Hetz Midget' is a dense, globular-shaped plant. It is a true dwarf, being perhaps the smallest form of *Thuja occidentalis*. Growth rate is very slow. A 10-year-old plant measured 10 to 14 inches high and 20 inches wide. Texture is medium.

The branches are rather stout.

The light-green leaves are tightly packed in sprays and turn bronze in the autumn.

Thuja occidentalis 'Hetz Midget' grows best in a deep, moist, well-drained soil with full sun and high humidity, but will grow in a marshy or limestone soil. The plant tolerates pruning. It is susceptible to damage from strong winds, snow, and ice, and is subject to attack from bagworms and the two-spotted mite.

Thuja occidentalis 'Hetz Midget' may be used in the foundation planting, a permanent landscape container, or as a specimen plant. *Thuja occidentalis* 'Minima' is similar to *Thuja occidentalis* 'Hetz Midget'.

This plant was found as a chance seedling in the Fairview Evergreen Nursery, Fairview, Pennsylvania, about 1928.

Cupressaceae (Cypress family)

Zone 5

Holmstrup's Eastern Arborvitae

May also be listed as *Thuja occidentalis holmstrupii, Thuja occidentalis holmstrupensis*

Thuja occidentalis 'Holmstrup' is a sturdy, dense, compact, narrowly pyramidal conifer with a strong trunk and central leader. Its ultimate size is 5 feet high and about 2 feet wide at the base. Growth rate is slow. Texture is medium.

The foliage is arranged in dense, flattened sprays typical of the *Thuja occidentalis* species. These sprays overlap and radiate in a vertical plane from the trunk. The leaves retain their rich apple-green color except during severe winters, when they usually turn brown.

Thuja occidentalis 'Holmstrup' grows best in a deep, moist, well-drained soil with full sun and high humidity, but will grow in a marshy or limestone soil. Annual pruning keeps the plant more compact and gives it a symmetrical outline. It is susceptible to damage from strong winds, snow, and ice, and is subject to attack from bagworms and the two-spotted mite.

This plant is one of the few dwarf cultivars with a conical habit. It may be used in a formal garden, permanent landscape container, or as a specimen plant, and is a good substitute for *Chamaecyparis obtusa* cultivars in areas where the latter are not hardy.

Thuja occidentalis 'Holmstrup' was first grown by A. M. Jensen, Holmstrup, Denmark, in 1951.

Cupressaceae (Cypress family)   Green Glove Eastern Arborvitae

Zone 5

Thuja occidentalis 'Little Gem' is a dense, compact, flattened, globose, broad shrub with an untidy appearance because of the characteristic twisting of the sprays and branchlets. Growth rate is slow. A 10-year-old plant measured 1 foot 3 inches high and 6 feet in diameter. Texture is medium.

The branches are thin, horizontal, and spreading, and the branchlets are rather crimped.

The glossy, dark-green leaves are arranged in crumpled, crowded sprays. The leaves are conspicuously glandular on both sides. The sprays are quite flat, and are held at various angles, giving the plant a dense appearance. The foliage holds its rich green color well, becoming somewhat darker in the winter.

Thuja occidentalis 'Little Gem' grows best in a deep, moist, well-drained soil with full sun and high humidity, but will grow in a marshy or limestone soil. The plant tolerates pruning. It is susceptible to damage from strong winds, snow, and ice, and is subject to attack from bagworms and the two-spotted mite.

Thuja occidentalis 'Little Gem' is one of the few true dwarfs of the *Thuja* species, and among the best dwarf cultivars. It may be used in the foundation planting, rock garden, a small, informal hedge, a permanent landscape container, or as a specimen plant. This plant is similar to *Thuja occidentalis* 'Pumila'.

Cupressaceae (Cypress family)

Zone 5

Recurva Nana Eastern Arborvitae

May also be listed as *Thuja occidentalis recurva nana*

Thuja occidentalis 'Recurva Nana' is a dense, low-growing, flat-topped, dome-shaped shrub with uniform growth. There seems to be more than one form of this plant. Its ultimate size is 4½ to 6 feet high and 4 feet wide. Growth rate is medium. Texture is medium.

The branches are erect and spread horizontally. The branchlets are noticeably recurved (half-turned) at the tips.

The foliage is quite flattened, uniform in width, and borne in crowded sprays. The sprays are usually held nearly horizontal, with each growing tip recurved and twisted. The leaves are green, turning brownish in winter.

Thuja occidentalis 'Recurva Nana' grows best in a deep, moist, well-drained soil with full sun and high humidity, but will grow in a marshy or limestone soil. The plant tolerates pruning. It is susceptible to damage from strong winds, snow, and ice, and is subject to attack from bagworms and the two-spotted mite.

This plant may be used in the foundation planting, rock garden, a small mass planting, a permanent landscape container, or as a specimen plant.

Cupressaceae (Cypress family)

Zone 5

Umbrella Eastern Arborvitae

May also be listed as *Thuja occidentalis umbraculifera*

Thuja occidentalis 'Umbraculifera' is a nearly globe-shaped shrub with branches extending to the ground. Growth rate is slow. A 10-year-old plant measured 2 feet 4 inches high and 3 feet wide. The ultimate height is about 3 to 4½ feet high. Texture is medium.

The plant has several main stems that spread out to support the dense, dome-shaped crown. The branchlets are erect and slightly curved, and the twigs are a conspicuous pinkish brown.

The fine, rich bluish-green leaves are borne in flat sprays. The shoots are irregularly flattened and daintily laid out and curved in the plane of the spray. The foliage turns dark bronzish green in winter.

Thuja occidentalis 'Umbraculifera' grows best in a deep, moist, well-drained soil with full sun and high humidity, but will grow in a marshy or limestone soil. It tolerates pruning. Because it does not transplant well, the plant should be moved when it is small. It is susceptible to damage from strong winds, snow, and ice, and is subject to attack from bagworms and the two-spotted mite.

This plant may be used in the foundation planting, rock garden, a mass planting, a permanent landscape container, or as a specimen plant.

Thuja occidentalis 'Umbraculifera' was first grown by Christopher Neder in Frankfort-on-Main, Germany, in the late 1800's.

Pinaceae (Pine family)

Zone 5

Bennett's Weeping Canadian Hemlock

May also be listed as *Tsuga canadensis* var. 'Bennett'

Tsuga canadensis 'Bennett' is a dense, spreading, crowded, low-growing conifer. Its ultimate size is about 4 feet high and 5 feet wide. Growth rate is slow. Texture is fine.

The branches are borne more or less horizontally. The twigs are slender, with secondary summer growth that is conspicuous, regular, and marked with short leaves that create a fanlike effect.

The medium-green leaves are about ⅓ inch long and closely set.

Tsuga canadensis 'Bennett' requires a moist, well-drained, acid soil. It grows well on rocky bluffs and in sandy soils, and tolerates shade. The plant will grow in full sun if there is adequate drainage and organic matter. It cannot tolerate wind, waterlogged soils, or polluted conditions. This plant is susceptible to sun scorch (the ends of the branches die back at temperatures in excess of 95° F.) and drouth injury during prolonged dry periods.

It may be used in the foundation planting, rock garden, a permanent landscape container, or as a specimen plant.

Tsuga canadensis 'Bennett' was first grown by M. Bennett, Atlantic Highlands, New Jersey, about 1920.

Pinaceae (Pine family)

Zone 5b

Cole's Canadian Hemlock, Cole's Prostrate
Canadian Hemlock

May also be listed as *Tsuga canadensis*
'Cole's Prostrate'

Tsuga canadensis 'Cole' may be grown naturally
as a prostrate shrub. It may also be grafted onto a
short standard or trained upwards when it is young so
that it assumes a weeping habit as it matures. If
untrained, the plant will grow 2 to 3 inches high and
2 to 3 feet wide. Growth rate is very slow. Texture
is fine.

The branches are long, slender, and lie flattened
along the ground, eventually forming extensive
carpets. The flattened main branches are nearly
without leaves in the center of the plant.

Tsuga canadensis 'Cole' requires a moist, well-
drained, acid soil. It grows well on rocky bluffs and
in sandy soils, and tolerates shade. The plant will grow
in full sun if there is adequate drainage and organic
matter. It cannot tolerate wind, waterlogged soils, or
polluted conditions. This plant is susceptible to sun
scorch (the ends of the branches die back at temperatures in excess of 95° F.) and drouth injury during
prolonged dry periods.

Tsuga canadensis 'Cole' may be used as a specimen
plant or in the rock garden. It flows gracefully over
and around rocks, following the contour of the ground.

H. R. Cole discovered this plant in 1929 near
the foot of Mt. Madison in New Hampshire. Cole
transplanted the original plant to the Gray and Cole
Nursery near Haverford, Massachusetts, where it
was propagated.

Pinaceae (Pine family)

Jeddeloh Canadian Hemlock

Zone 5

Tsuga canadensis 'Jeddeloh' is a compressed, squat bush, often with a depression in the center resembling a bird's nest. Growth rate is slow. A 10-year-old plant measured 1 foot 8 inches high and 3 feet wide. Texture is fine.

The foliage is a bright lime-green that is accentuated with the new growth in the spring.

Tsuga canadensis 'Jeddeloh' requires a moist, well-drained, acid soil. It grows well on rocky bluffs and in sandy soils, and tolerates shade. The plant will grow in full sun if there is adequate drainage and organic matter. It cannot tolerate wind, waterlogged soils, or polluted conditions. This plant is susceptible to sun scorch (the ends of the branches die back at temperatures in excess of 95° F.) and drouth injury during prolonged dry periods.

It may be used in the foundation planting, a mass planting, rock garden, or a permanent landscape container.

Tsuga canadensis 'Jeddeloh' originated in Europe.

For a color illustration of *Tsuga canadensis* 'Jeddeloh', see page 144.

Pinaceae (Pine family)   Lewis's Canadian Hemlock

Zone 5

Tsuga canadensis 'Lewisii' is an irregularly shaped, somewhat pyramidal conifer with stiff growth. Growth rate is very slow. A 12-year-old plant measured 2 feet 3 inches high and 1 foot 8 inches wide. Texture is fine.

The branches are somewhat sparse. The branchlets are crowded, with prominent leading shoots.

The dark-green leaves are long, broad, and crowded, and are borne erect.

Tsuga canadensis 'Lewisii' requires a moist, well-drained, acid soil. It grows well on rocky bluffs and in sandy soils, and tolerates shade. The plant will grow in full sun if there is adequate drainage and organic matter. It cannot tolerate wind, waterlogged soils, or polluted conditions. This plant is susceptible to sun scorch (the ends of the branches die back at temperatures in excess of 95° F.) and drouth injury during prolonged dry periods.

It may be used in the foundation planting, rock garden, a permanent landscape container, or as a specimen plant.

Pinaceae (Pine family)

Zone 5

Little Canadian Hemlock

May also be listed as *Tsuga canadensis minima*

Tsuga canadensis 'Minima' is a dainty, soft, rounded, spreading shrub with a many-tiered effect. It rarely exceeds 3 feet in height and 10 feet in width, and does not lose its shape with age. Growth rate is very slow. Texture is fine.

The branches arch and droop. The inner branches ascend at a low angle, and terminate in graceful sprays of slightly drooping foliage. The branchlets are short and arching.

The leaves are ¼ to ⅓ inch long and green on the upper sides, with 2 glaucous green bands that give the plant a grayish appearance.

Tsuga canadensis 'Minima' requires a moist, well-drained, acid soil. It grows well on rocky bluffs and in sandy soils, and tolerates shade. The plant will grow in full sun if there is adequate drainage and organic matter. It cannot tolerate wind, waterlogged soils, or polluted conditions. This plant is susceptible to sun scorch (the ends of the branches die back at temperatures in excess of 95° F.) and drouth injury during prolonged dry periods.

It may be used in the foundation planting, rock garden, a permanent landscape container, or as a specimen plant.

Tsuga canadensis 'Minima' was first grown by H. A. Hesse, Weener-on-Ems, Germany, and was introduced about 1890.

Color Illustrations

Chaenomeles japonica (flowers)
Japanese Flowering Quince
page 20

Cotoneaster horizontalis (fruit)
Rockspray, Rock Cotoneaster
page 23

Cytisus decumbens (flowers)
Prostrate Broom
page 24

Daphne cneorum (flowers)
Rose Daphne, Garland Flower
page 26

Deutzia gracilis
(flowers)
Slender Deutzia
page 28

Fothergilla gardenii (foliage)
Dwarf Fothergilla, Witch Alder
page 30

Hypericum frondosum 'Sunburst' (flowers)
Sunburst Golden St.-John's-wort
page 33

Philadelphus 'Silver Showers' (flowers)
Silver Showers Mockorange
page 38

Potentilla fruticosa 'Katherine Dykes'
(flowers)
Katherine Dykes Bush Cinquefoil,
Katherine Dykes Potentilla
page 40

Spiraea × bumalda 'Anthony Waterer' (flowers)
Anthony Waterer Spirea
page 47

Spiraea × bumalda 'Goldflame' (foliage)
Goldflame Spirea
page 49

Arctostaphylos uva-ursi (flowers)
Bearberry, Kinnikinick, Mealberry,
Mountain Box
page 59

Mahonia aquifolium 'Compactum' (fruit)
Compact Oregon Hollygrape, Compact Oregon Grapeholly
page 70

Mahonia repens (flowers)
Creeping Mahonia,
Creeping Hollygrape, Ash Barberry
page 71

Rhododendron 'Boule de Neige'
Boule de Neige Rhododendron
page 79

Rhododendron 'Herbert'
Herbert's Azalea
page 80

Rhododendron impeditum
Cloudland Rhododendron
page 81

Rhododendron 'Karens'
Karens Azalea
page 82

Rhododendron ✕ *laetevirens*
Wilson Rhododendron
page 83

Rhododendron 'Pioneer'
Pioneer Rhododendron
page 83

Rhododendron 'P.J.M.'
P.J.M. Rhododendron
page 84

Rhododendron 'Purple Gem'
Purple Gem Rhododendron
page 85

Rhododendron 'Ramapo'
Ramapo Rhododendron
page 85

Rhododendron 'Stewartstonian'
Stewart's Azalea
page 86

Rhododendron 'Windbeam'
Windbeam Rhododendron
page 86

Rhododendron yakusimanum
Yak Rhododendron
page 87

'Yaku Prince' (cultivar)

Rhododendron yeodoense var. *poukhanense*
Korean Azalea
page 88

flowers

Juniperus conferta (male flowers)
Shore Juniper
page 104

Juniperus procumbens 'Nana' (foliage)
Dwarf Japgarden Juniper
page 108

Picea pungens 'Globosa'
Globe Colorado Spruce
page 117

Tsuga canadensis 'Jeddeloh'
Jeddeloh Canadian Hemlock
page 134

Glossary

Index

Botanical Names of Plants
Common Names of Plants

List of Publications

Glossary

achene

needle-shaped leaf

alternate leaves

awl-shaped leaf

campanulate flower

capsule

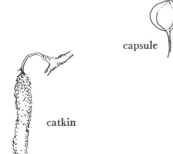

catkin

Abscission. The natural separation of leaves, flowers, and fruits from the plant.

Achene. A small, dry, 1-seeded fruit that remains closed at maturity.

Acicular. A needle-shaped leaf.

Alternate. Leaves arranged singly at different heights and on different sides of the stem.

Anther. The pollen-bearing part of a stamen; usually borne at the top of the filament. See illustration, page 152.

Apetalous. A flower composed without petals.

Appressed. Pressed close to the stem.

Arborescent. Resembling a tree; of treelike habit.

Awl-shaped. Tapering gradually to a stiff, fine point, as an awl-shaped leaf.

Axil. Angular space between a leaf and the stem. See illustration of a zigzag stem, page 151.

Axillary. Situated in an axil.

Basal. Leaves arising from the base of a stem.

Bilabiate. 2-lipped; often applied to the corolla or calyx.

Bloom. See Glaucous.

Bract. A leaf borne on a floral axis. See illustration, page 152.

Calyx. The leafy part of a flower composed of fused sepals that are usually green but can be petallike. See illustration, page 152.

Campanulate. Bell-shaped.

Capsule. A dry, usually many-seeded fruit that arises from a compound pistil and splits open along 2 or more sutures.

Catkin. A spikelike inflorescence that resembles a cat's tail in shape, as in the birch tree or willow.

Columnar. Resembling a column in form; a straight, narrow habit of certain trees and shrubs. See illustration, page 153.

Complete flower. A flower with all 4 floral structures: sepals, petals, stamens, and pistils. See illustration, page 152.

compound leaves

drupe

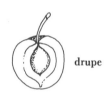

entire leaf

falcate leaf

follicle

Compound leaf. A leaf composed of 2 or more leaflets on a common petiole.

Corolla. The fused petals of a flower. See illustration, page 152.

Corymb. A more or less flat-topped, indeterminate inflorescence in which the outer flowers open first. See illustration, page 154.

Cyme. A determinate inflorescence, usually broad and more or less flat-topped, in which the central or terminal flower opens first. See illustration, page 154.

Cymose. Arranged in cymes; cymelike.

Decumbent. Reclining on the ground but with ascending tips.

Deflexed. Bent abruptly downward or backward.

Determinate. A type of inflorescence in which the stem ceases to grow after the plant flowers.

Dimorphic. Occurring in 2 forms.

Dioecious. Having the staminate (male) and pistillate (female) flowers on different plants.

Dormant. Not actively growing but protected from the environment; usually a winter condition.

Drupe. A fleshy, 1-seeded fruit, such as a cherry or plum; a stone fruit.

Entire leaf. A leaf whose margin does not have teeth or indentations.

Espalier. A plant trained to grow flat against a wall or trellis.

Exfoliate. To peel off in thin layers.

Falcate leaf. A sickle-shaped leaf.

Fascicle. A compact bundle or cluster of leaves.

Fastigiate. With erect branches that are close together. See illustration, page 153.

Filament. The stalk that bears the anther in a stamen. See illustration, page 152.

Filiform. Long and slender; threadlike.

Follicle. A dry, many-seeded fruit that arises from a simple pistil and splits open along only 1 suture.

Floriferous. Bearing many flowers.

Glabrous. Without hairs; smooth.

Glaucous. Covered with a "bloom" (a white or pale blue powdery or waxy coating that rubs off easily, as in the grape or plum).

Globose. Having a round or spherical shape. See illustration, page 153.

Herbaceous. A plant that has little or no woody tissue and dies back to the ground each year.

Hose-in-hose. A double flower in which 1 flower appears to be inside the other; occasionally occurs in *Rhododendron*.

Hybrid. A plant resulting from a cross between 2 distinct species, subspecies, or varieties.

Hybridize. To produce hybrids; crossbreed.

Imbricated. To overlap, as shingles on a roof.

Imperfect flower. A flower with either stamens or pistils but not both.

Incomplete flower. A flower that lacks 1 or more of the 4 floral structures: sepals, petals, stamens, and pistils.

Indeterminate. A type of inflorescence in which the stem continues to grow after the plant flowers.

Indumentum. A dense covering of hairs.

Inflorescence. The arrangement of flowers on a stem; the flowering of a plant. See illustrations, page 154.

Midrib. The central vein of a leaf.

Monoecious. Having the staminate (male) and pistillate (female) flowers on the same plant.

Node. A joint or point on a stem at which a leaf or leaves are attached. See illustration of a typical stem, page 151.

Opposite. Leaves arranged in pairs at different heights on a stem, each separated from the other by ½ the circumference of the stem.

Ovary. The rounded, usually basal part of the pistil that bears the ovules. See illustration, page 152.

Ovule. The egg-containing unit of the ovary that becomes the seed after fertilization.

Palmate. A compound leaf in which 3 or more leaflets arise from a common point.

Panicle. An indeterminate inflorescence with repeated branching of spikes, racemes, corymbs, or umbels. See illustration, page 154.

Pedicle (Pedicel). The stalk of an individual flower. See illustration, page 152.

Peduncle. The primary stalk of a flower or flower cluster. See illustration, page 152.

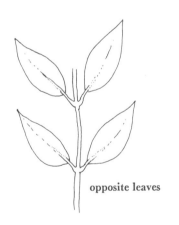

opposite leaves

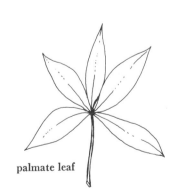

palmate leaf

pinnate leaf

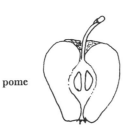

pome

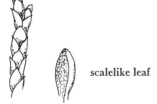

scalelike leaf

serrate leaf

simple leaf

Perfect flower. A flower with both stamens and pistils. See illustration, page 152.

Persistent. Remaining attached, as of a leaf.

Petiole. The stalk of a leaf. See illustration of a zigzag stem, page 151.

Pinnate. A compound leaf in which the leaflets arise on each side of a common axis.

Pistil. The female part of a flower, comprising ovary, style, and stigma. See illustration, page 152.

Pistillate. Having pistils but no stamens.

Pith. The spongy tissue in the stem of a plant. See illustration of a typical stem, page 151.

Pollination. The transfer of pollen from a stamen to a pistil.

Pome. A fleshy fruit, such as the apple, composed of an outer fleshy layer and a central core with seeds enclosed in a capsule.

Pubescent. Covered with soft, short hairs.

Pulvinus (plural pulvini). A minute gland or an enlargement at the base of a petiole.

Pyramidal. Pyramid-shaped, with a pointed top and sloping sides. See illustration, page 153.

Raceme. An unbranched, indeterminate inflorescence in which the flowers are borne in short pedicles along a central axis. See illustration, page 154.

Recurved. Curved backward or downward.

Revolute. Rolled backward and downward, as the margins of leaves.

Rhizome. A usually horizontal underground stem that produces leafy shoots above and roots below.

Rosette. A circular cluster of leaves resembling the shape of a rose.

Scalelike leaf. A small, clasping leaf resembling a scale.

Sepal. One of the leaves of a calyx. See illustration, page 152.

Serrate leaf. Saw-toothed leaf, with the teeth pointing forward or toward the apex.

Sessile. Without a stalk.

Simple leaf. A leaf that is not compound (not divided into leaflets).

Spike. An elongated inflorescence in which the flowers are sessile (borne without stems) along the axis. See illustration, page 154.

stipule

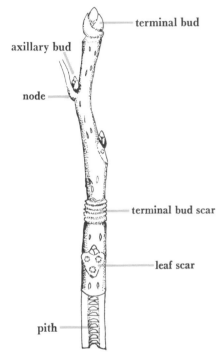

terminal bud

axillary bud

node

terminal bud scar

leaf scar

pith

Typical Stem

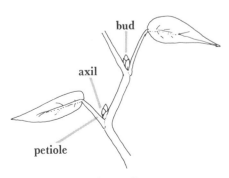

bud

axil

petiole

Zigzag Stem

Spine. A stiff, sharp, pointed outgrowth from a leaf, leaf part, or stem.

Stamen. The pollen-bearing organ of a seed plant, typically consisting of an anther and a filament. See illustration, page 152.

Staminate. Having stamens but no pistils.

Stigma. The portion of a flower pistil that receives pollen grains and on which they germinate. See illustration, page 152.

Stipule. Either of a pair of lateral appendages at the base of a leaf.

Stolon. A horizontal stem that runs along the ground and roots at the nodes, producing new plants.

Stoloniferous. Bearing stolons.

Stomate (plural stomata). A pore or minute opening in the surface of a leaf or stem through which gases are exchanged.

Style. A long, slender extension of the ovary that bears a stigma at its apex. See illustration, page 152.

Subtend. To occupy an adjacent and lower position to another structure and often enclosing it, as a bract subtending a flower.

Subterminal. Situated near but not at an end.

Tap root. The primary descending root of a plant.

Terete. Circular in cross-section.

Terminal. Growing at the end of a branch or stem.

Topiary. Training, cutting, and trimming shrubs and trees into odd or ornamental shapes.

Transpiration. The emission of water vapor from the surfaces of leaves.

Truss. A compact flower cluster. See illustrations of *Rhododendron* flowers, pages 79-88.

Umbel. An indeterminate, usually flat-topped or convex inflorescence in which the pedicles of the flowers arise from a common point, resembling the framework of an umbrella. See illustration, page 154.

Umbellate. Resembling an umbel; umbrella-shaped. See illustration, page 154.

Urceolate. Urn-shaped. See illustration, page 153.

Vein. One of the vascular bundles comprising the framework of a leaf.

Zigzag stem. Bent back and forth at the nodes. See illustration.

Flowers

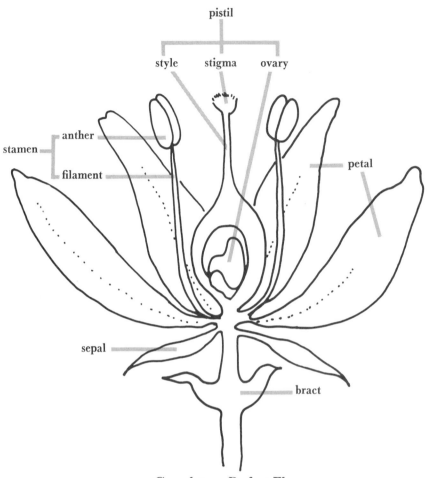

Complete or Perfect Flower

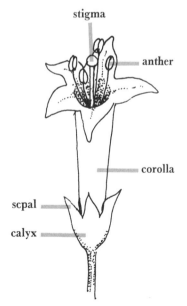

Tubular-shaped Flower

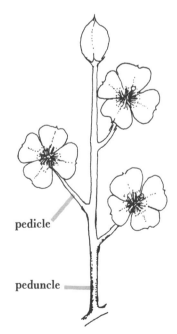

Growth Habits

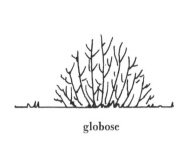

globose

urceolate

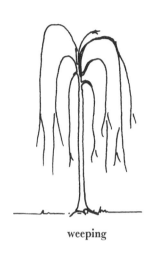

weeping

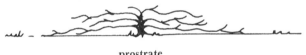

prostrate

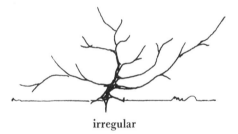

irregular

fastigiate

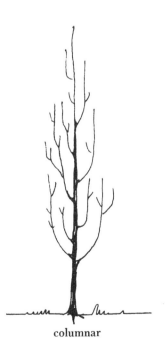

columnar

pyramidal

Inflorescence

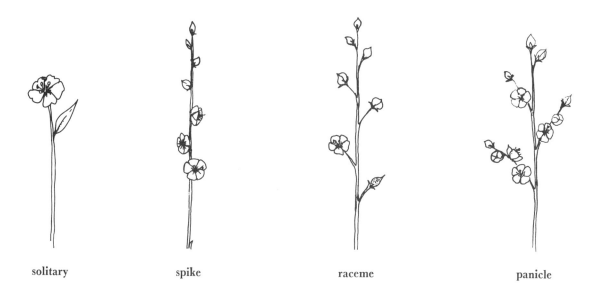

solitary   spike   raceme   panicle

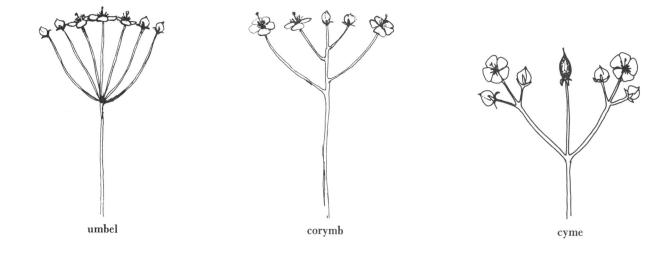

umbel   corymb   cyme

Index
Botanical Names of Plants

Index
Common Names of Plants

List of Publications

The following publications provide more comprehensive discussions of the plants described in this book. You may also obtain additional information from your county Cooperative Extension office, state land-grant university, the U.S. Department of Agriculture, and nationally recognized arboretums and botanic gardens.

Bean, W.J. *Trees and Shrubs Hardy in the British Isles.* 8th ed. 3 vols. London: John Murray, 1973.

Bowers, Clement G. *Rhododendrons and Azaleas.* New York: Macmillan Publishing Co., 1960.

Carter, J. Cedric. *Diseases of Midwest Trees.* Special Publication 35. University of Illinois at Urbana-Champaign College of Agriculture in cooperation with Illinois Natural History Survey, 1975.

Christopher, Everett P. *The Pruning Manual.* New York: Macmillan Publishing Co., 1954.

Cox, Peter A. *Dwarf Rhododendrons.* New York: Macmillan Publishing Co., 1973.

Dallimore, W., and A. Bruce Jackson. *A Handbook of Coniferae and Ginkgoaceae.* Revised by S.G. Harrison. New York: St. Martin's Press, 1967.

Dirr, Michael A. *Manual of Woody Landscape Plants: Their Identification, Characteristics, Culture, Propagation and Uses.* Champaign, Illinois: Stipes Publishing Co., 1977.

Giles, F.A., and W.B. Siefert. *Pruning and Care of Evergreens and Deciduous Trees and Shrubs.* Circular 1033. University of Illinois at Urbana-Champaign College of Agriculture Cooperative Extension Service, 1971.

Harrison, Charles R. *Ornamental Conifers.* New York: Hafner Press, 1975.

Hartmann, Hudson T., and Dale E. Kester. *Plant Propagation: Principles and Practices.* 3rd ed. Englewood Cliffs, New Jersey: Prentice-Hall, 1975.

Hillier, H.G. *Hillier's Manual of Trees and Shrubs.* Newton Abbott, Devon, England: David and Charles, 1975.

Hornibrook, Murray. *Dwarf and Slow-Growing Conifers.* 2nd ed. New York: Charles Scribner's Sons, 1938.

Hortus Third. Staff of the L.H. Bailey Hortorium. Cornell University. New York: Macmillan Publishing Co., 1979.

Leach, David G. *Rhododendrons of the World and How to Grow Them.* New York: Charles Scribner's Sons, 1961.

Nelson, William R., Jr. *Landscaping Your Home.* Circular 1111. rev. ed. University of Illinois at Urbana-Champaign College of Agriculture Cooperative Extension Service, 1975.

Ouden, Pieter den, and B.K. Boom. *Manual of Cultivated Cultivars.* The Hague: Martinus Nijhoff, 1965.

Reisch, Kenneth W., Philip C. Kozel, and Gayle A. Weinstein. *Woody Ornamentals for the Midwest.* The Ohio State University. Dubuque, Iowa: Kendall/Hunt Publishing Co., 1975.

Seeds of Woody Plants in the United States. Agriculture Handbook No. 450. Washington, D.C.: U.S. Department of Agriculture Forest Service, 1974.

Spangler, Ronald L., and Jerry Ripperda. *Landscape Plants for the Central and Northeastern U.S., Including Lower and Eastern Canada.* Michigan State University. Minneapolis, Minnesota: Burgess Publishing Co., 1977.

Welch, H.J. *Dwarf Conifers.* London: Faber and Faber, 1968.

Wyman, Donald. *Dwarf Shrubs.* New York: Macmillan Publishing Co., 1975.

Wyman, Donald. *Ground Cover Plants.* New York: Macmillan Publishing Co., 1956.

Wyman, Donald. *Shrubs and Vines for American Gardens.* New York: Macmillan Publishing Co., 1969.

Zucker, Isabel. *Flowering Shrubs.* Princeton, New Jersey: D. Van Nostrand Co., 1966.